Basic Concept Stories

Written by: Beverly Foster
Edited by: M. Thomas Webber, Jr. & Christina L. Haislip M.S., CCC-SLP
Illustrated by:
Julie Bunner, Chuck Hart, Steve Barr, Tony Mitchell,
Chris Parker, Chris Turner, David Kramer & Tawnia Lechner

www.superduperinc.com
1-800-277-8737

ISBN 978-1-58650-080-1

Dedication

To Steve,
a “super duper” friend.
Thanks
for supporting me
in all my endeavors!

Acknowledgment

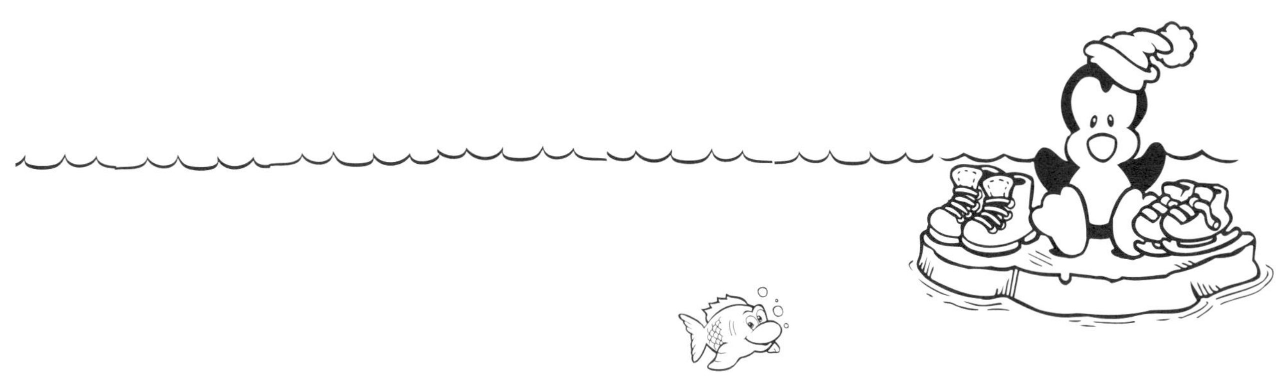

I'd like to thank
all the dedicated
Language, Speech, and
Hearing Specialists
in the Elk Grove
Unified School District!

Contents

Introduction

The *Fold and Say® Book* is designed to be a fun way to reinforce the student's correct production of basic concepts. Fill out the parent letter and send it home with the student along with the student's *Fold and Say®* stories. Be sure to fill in the target concept and then check off the specific practice exercise(s) that you wish the child to do at home. The exercises address all phases of student language therapy - listening only, or practice of the concept at word level and at sentence level. The parent letter can be signed and returned as the homework sheet, so that the student may keep the *Fold and Say®* book(s) at home for further practice or as a keepsake.

Some of the activities listed in the parent letter can also be done in the therapy sessions. At the end of the parent letter is a space for you to add your own therapy activity as suits your student's needs and your teaching style.

Activity suggestions:

1. Read the story to the student, emphasizing the basic concept.
2. Read the story aloud to the student, leaving out the basic concept and having them fill in the blanks.
3. Have each student read a page. Or, have one student read a page, leaving out the basic concept, and have the next student fill in the blank.
4. Have your students act out the story, including the dialogue where applicable.
5. Copy a second sheet of the story and have the students cut apart the four pages. Then, have the students paste the story in its correct sequence on construction paper to create a sequence story.
6. Have your student say the story backwards, from the last page to the first.
7. Ask your students questions designed to get the basic concept as an answer. For example, ask "What word in your story rhymes with two?" to get the answer "through."
8. Tell your student you are thinking of a word in the story. Have the students guess the the word you are thinking of by asking questions that you can answer only "yes" or "no."
9. For a more conversational level, ask your student what happened before the story or what they think might happen next in the story.
10. Have the student fill in other ways to use the basic concept in a sentence. For example, "I can go **in** a __________." (car, train, box, etc.)

Dear Parent/Helper: Date____________________

An integral part of your child's speech program is continuing to reinforce the skills they have learned by having speech practice at home. Your child will be bringing home a Fold and Say story for use in practice of his/her *basic concept*. The *Basic Concept* is the concept such as "*in*," "*on*," "*under*," "*over*," etc. that your child is presently working on in speech and language therapy. Below is a list of activities to be done using the Fold and Say Story. Please complete these exercises with your child, and then, sign, date and return this note. Give plenty of encouragement and praise, and above all, make these activities fun!

Your child's Basic Concept is : ________________________________.

- ❑ Read the story to your child, emphasizing the basic concept.
- ❑ Read the story with your child, alternating pages.
- ❑ Have your child read the story to you.
- ❑ Read the story to your child, leaving the basic concept for your child to fill in.
- ❑ Ask your child to use the basic concept in a separate sentence. For example, "I can go ***in*** a ________ ." (car, boat, box, etc.)
- ❑ Have your child continue the Fold and Say story. Ask what your child thinks would happen next in the story. Have him/her draw a picture to go with his/her ideas.
- ❑ Have your child read the story out loud "backwards" - in reverse order.
- ❑ Ask your child questions designed to get the basic concept as an answer. For example, ask "What word in your story rhymes with *two*?" to get the answer "t*hrough*."
- ❑ Have your child make up a silly story using the basic concept. Have them draw their story idea.
- ❑ During the day, emphasize the basic concept whenever possible. For example, if you are at the grocery store, you can have him/her put the fruit **in** a bag, groceries **in** the cart, etc.
- ❑ ____
  ____

Thank you for your support,

________________________ ________________________

Speech-Language Pathologist Parent/Helper's Signature Date

same

different

Basic Concept Stories!

down

up

Bumble the Bee

Bumble the Bee lived in a beehive **above** the ground.

Bumble and his friends liked to fly **above** the hive.

One day they flew **above** the big old tree.

Bumble and his friends also loved flying **above** the flowers.

1 2 3 4

Cut on dotted line

Cut on dotted line

Clarence the Clown

At the circus, Clarence the Clown juggled three balls **above** his stool.

That was too easy, so he stood on the stool and juggled the balls **above** the ringmaster's head.

While riding his bike, he continued juggling the balls **above** the handle bars.

The crowd enjoyed the show and ...d loudly with their hands **above**

Rosa's New Friend

After getting off the bus, Rosa had to go to the office.

After knocking several times, she decided to open the door.

Matthew was waiting. He was new at school. **After** Rosa said, "hi," they shook hands.

After the bell rang, Rosa walked to class with her new friend.

1 2 3 4

Cut on dotted line

Cut on dotted line

Kyle told Leon, "We can play **after** we finish our homework."

The children rode home on their bikes, and Leon ran **after** them.

Chasing After Leon

Everyone played together **after** dinner.

After school, Leon the Leprechaun wanted to play with the children.

Renee and Judy

At camp, Renee and Judy noticed their backpacks were **alike**.

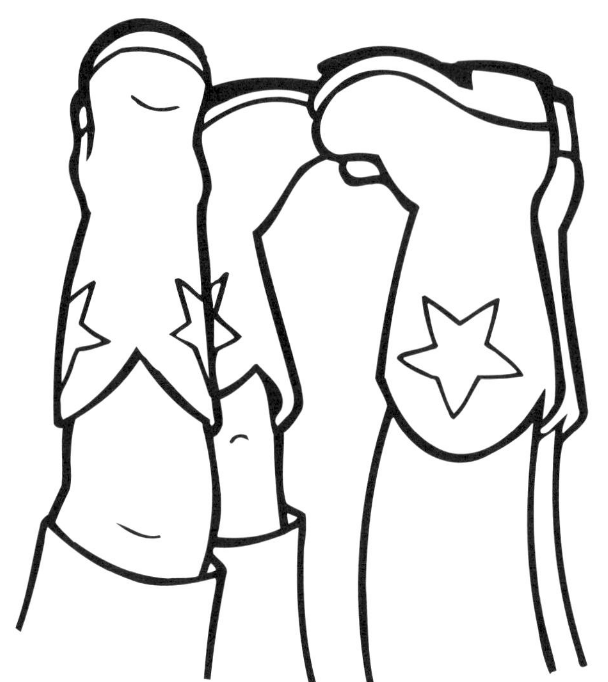

Then they looked at their boots and they were **alike** too.

Both girls noticed their sleeping bags were **alike**.

They looked at each other and laughed. They even giggled **alike**.

Cut on dotted line

Cut on dotted line

Desmond and Douglas

Desmond and Douglas were twins that looked **alike**.

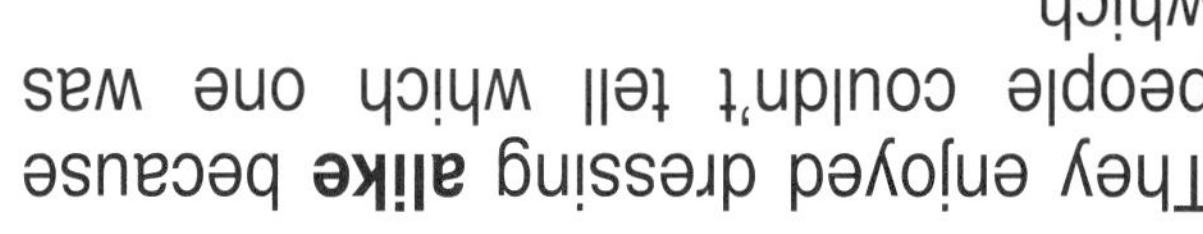

They enjoyed dressing **alike** because people couldn't tell which one was which.

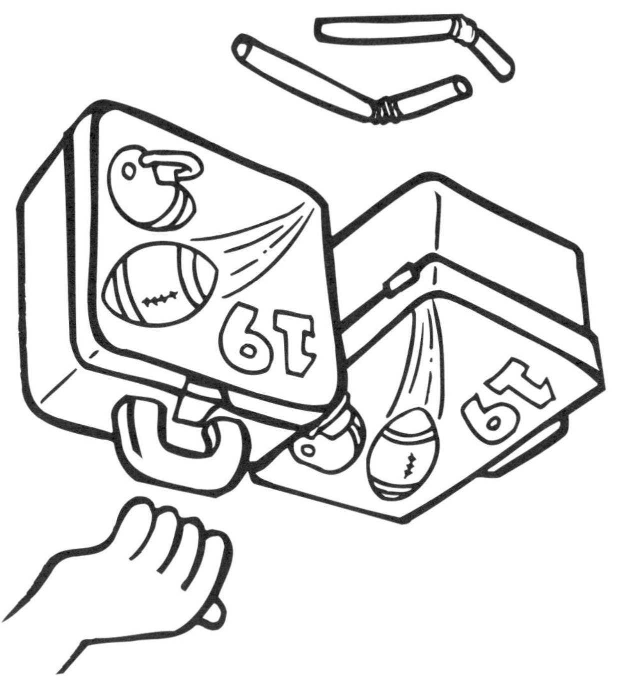

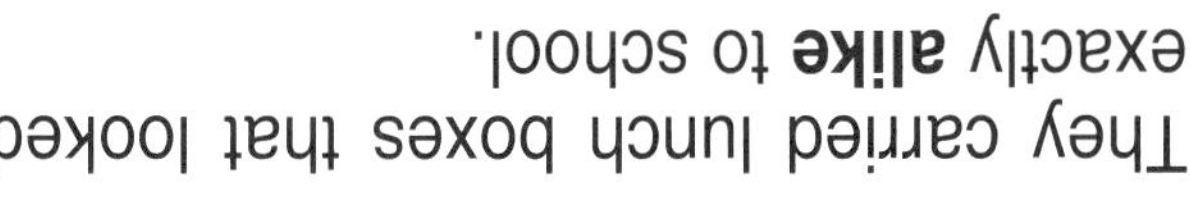

They carried lunch boxes that looked exactly **alike** to school.

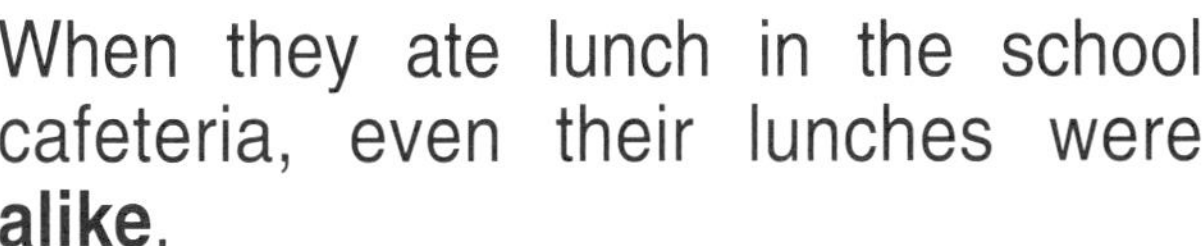

When they ate lunch in the school cafeteria, even their lunches were **alike**.

A Trip to the Aquarium

All of Cathy's family went to the aquarium.

They saw **all** four dolphins jump through giant hoops.

When the whale slapped its tail on the water, they **all** got wet.

At the end of the day, **all** of them were sad to leave the aquarium.

Cut on dotted line

Teddy Bears' Picnic

The teddy bears were preparing a picnic lunch. First, they packed **all** their food in a basket.

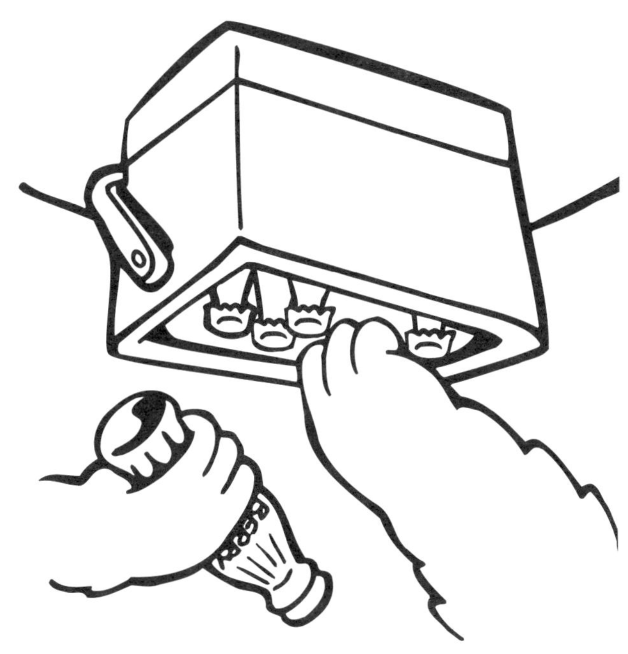

Then, they packed **all** the drinks in a cooler.

Carrying the basket and cooler, **all** the teddy bears walked to the park.

When they reached the park, they **all** ate lunch near a big tree.

Cut on dotted line

Always

Miguel and Juan were friends. They were **always** together.

On warm summer days, they **always** went to the pool.

After swimming, they **always** rode home on their bikes.

Then, they **always** ate dinner and read books together.

Cut on dotted line

Brenda the Bear

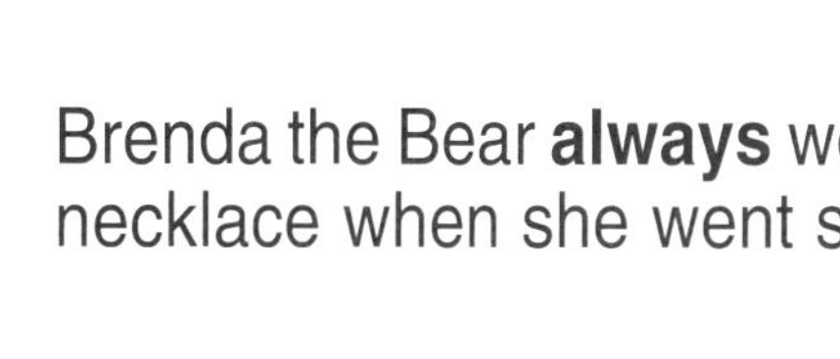

Brenda the Bear **always** wore her lucky necklace when she went shopping.

On Tuesdays, Brenda went to the market and **always** bought two jars of honey.

After shopping, she **always** went straight home to make honey cookies.

For Brenda, the best part of the day was **always** eating what she made. Yum!

Around her ankles, she wore two shiny anklets.

Around her wrist, she wore a charm bracelet.

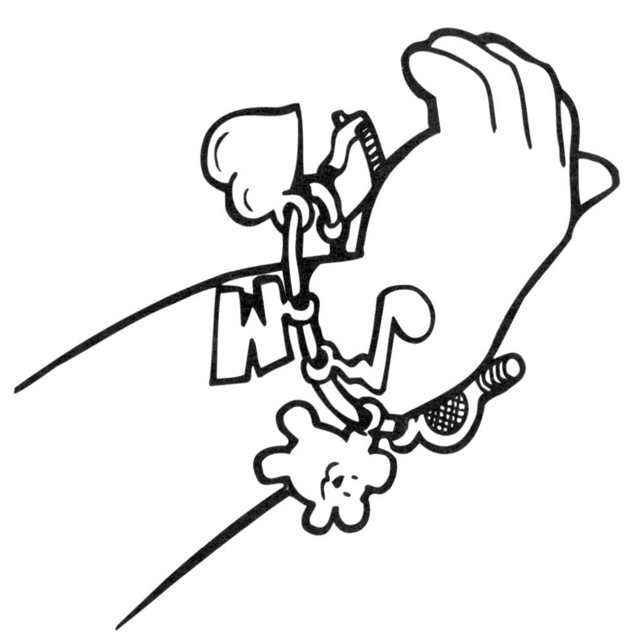

3 2
4 1

Covered in Jewelry

Then she put a belt **around** her waist. "Just right," said Monika.

Monika wore a beautiful heart-shaped necklace **around** her neck.

Cut on dotted line

Cut on dotted line

Josh Goes to the Fair

At the fair, Josh loved going **around** on the ferris wheel.

When he was on the ferris wheel, he put his arms **around** his father's neck.

His favorite game was throwing hoops **around** toys.

When his hoop landed **around** a stuffed tiger, Josh got to keep it !

Cut on dotted line

A Fun Field Trip

Stacy sat in the **back** of the bus on the class field trip to the farm.

At the farm, she quietly stood in **back** of Farmer Frank as he milked the cow.

The class saw many pigs in **back** of the barn.

Stacy waited in **back** of the line as the kids boarded the bus. She had a wonderful field trip!

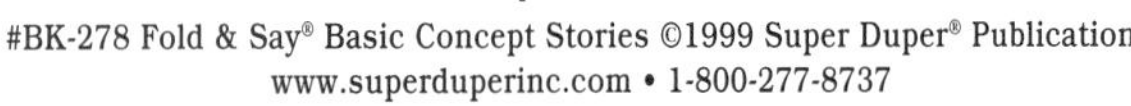

Cut on dotted line

Back Yard Chores

Jeremy and Joey had to finish their chores in the **back** of the house before going to a hockey game.

Both boys ran out of the **back** door and quickly went to work.

Jeremy painted the **back** of the fence while Joey pulled the weeds in **back** of the swingset.

When they were done, the boys jumped into the **back** seat of their mother's car to go to the game.

Cut on dotted line

Zelda Gets Loose

One day, Zelda the Snake escaped from the **back** of her cage.

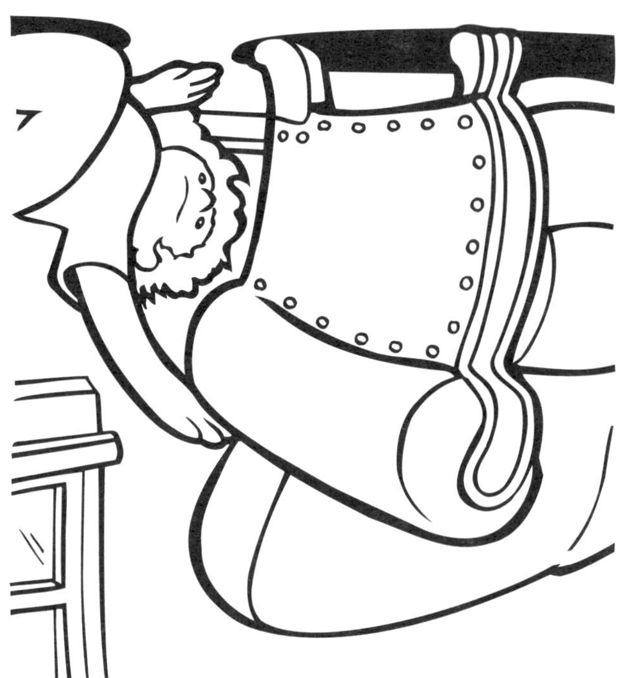

Lucy, her owner, looked for Zelda in the **back** of the couch.

Then she checked in **back** of the china cabinet, but still no sign of Zelda.

From the **back** of the house, Lucy's mom screamed loudly. "I guess Mom found Zelda for me," Lucy said.

1 2 3 4

Cut on dotted line

Hide and Go Seek

Randy played hide and go seek with his friends in **back** of the school.

He first hid in **back** of the old oak tree.

Later he hid behind the **back** of the slide.

His best friend walked in **back** of him, tapped him on the arm, and said, "You're it!"

Cut on dotted line

Marvin's Day

In the morning, Marvin put on his pants **before** he put on his shirt.

Then, he ate his cereal **before** he drank his juice.

He put on his backpack **before** he left the house.

At the bus stop, Marvin let his friend Mary get on the bus **before** him.

Stella the Spider

Stella the Spider did her exercises **before** eating lunch.

Then, she made a big web **before** she took a nap.

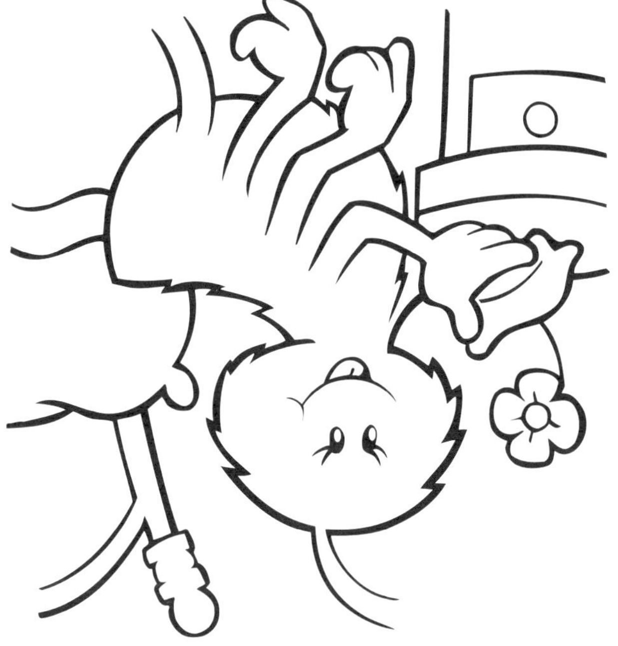

She took off her cap **before** she went to bed.

Before she fell asleep, she thought about her busy day.

Cut on dotted line

Beginning the Day

It was the **beginning** of a beautiful day in the forest.

Sam the Squirrel was **beginning** to climb the oak tree when he heard a tiny cry.

Molly the Squirrel was **beginning** to bury her acorns, but caught a splinter in her paw.

Sam pulled out the splinter. This was the **beginning** of a beautiful friendship.

Cut on dotted line

Cut on dotted line

Beginning of Summer

Travis woke up and knew it was the **beginning** of a great summer vacation.

He was **beginning** to read books all by himself.

He was also **beginning** to ride his two wheeler bike without the training wheels!

Travis showed how big he was by **beginning** to do his chores without any help!

1 2 3 4

Behind the School

Nicky and Ken loved to play on the swings **behind** the school.

Ken would get **behind** Nicky and push her.

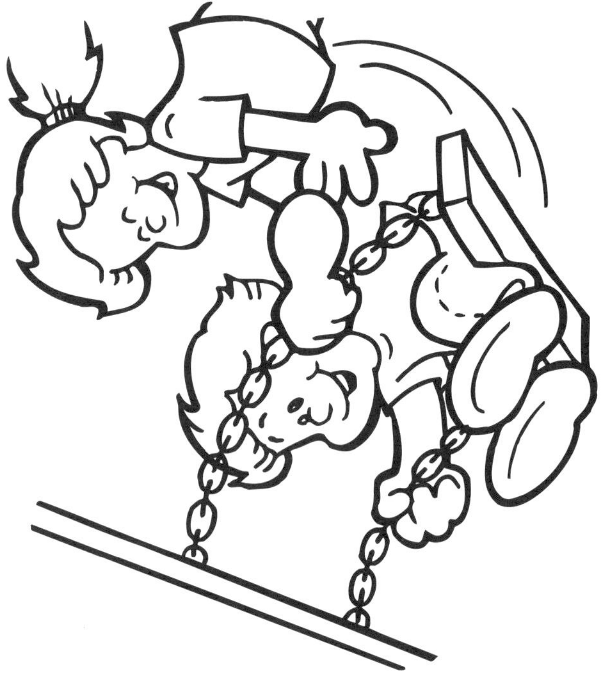

Nicky would get **behind** Ken and push him.

They both loved the way their hair would blow **behind** them when they went forward.

1 2 3 4

Cut on dotted line

The County Fair

Amy went to the County Fair **behind** the movie theater.

She walked **behind** the great big ferris wheel to the other rides.

She sat **behind** her friend Tommy on the roller coaster ride.

After the rides, Amy met Tommy **behind** the popcorn cart. It was a wonderful day at the Fair!

Cut on dotted line

Taking Pictures

Rodesha stood **behind** her new camera ready to take pictures.

She snapped a picture of her kitten peeking out from **behind** a flower pot.

Then she took a picture of her sister standing **behind** her wagon.

Rodesha finished up by taking many pictures of the flowers **behind** her house. What a beautiful day!

1 2 3 4

Cut on dotted line

Cut on dotted line

The Bakery

Mrs. Wilson worked **behind** the food counter at the bakery.

She put the fresh doughnuts in the case **behind** the cakes.

Little Lauren stood **behind** her Mom and anxiously waited for a doughnut.

Mrs. Wilson had a special doughnut **behind** her back especially for Lauren. What a surprise!

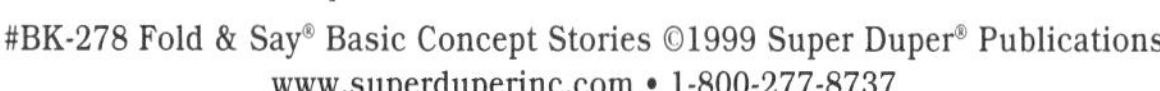

Cut on dotted line

Below Ocean Waves

Mike and Stephanie were turtles who loved to swim **below** the ships in the ocean.

They often swam **below** whales and **below** sharks passing by.

One day Mike got stuck **below** a big rock and couldn't get out.

Stephanie pushed the rock over and set Mike free. They swam away **below** a school of fish!

Cut on dotted line

Squeakers the Mouse

Squeakers the Mouse lived in a small mouse hole **below** the kitchen sink.

He gathered the food crumbs he found **below** the kitchen table in a sack.

Squeakers carried the food to a shelf **below** the kitchen window.

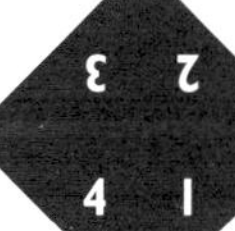

Squeakers would swing his feet **below** the shelf as he sat and ate his lunch.

Maria's Pumpkin

It was Halloween and Maria went to the pumpkin patch **beside** the Haunted House.

As she walked through the pumpkin patch, she spotted a cute little pumpkin **beside** the oak tree.

She decided to look for a larger pumpkin and found one **beside** the scarecrow.

Maria carved her pumpkin and placed it **beside** her front door for everyone to see.

Cut on dotted line

Rock and Roll Band

Marybeth stood **beside** Sarah to sing while Sarah played a rock and roll song.

Anthony joined them, and played his guitar **beside** them.

The music was so loud that Marybeth's Mom told them to practice in the garage **beside** the house.

Daisy joined the band and played her drums **beside** Anthony. The four musicians sounded terrific!

1 2 3 4

Cut on dotted line

Cut on dotted line

Sitting Between Friends

Bill went to see a space movie and sat **between** his two good friends.

He went to the snack bar and saw the popcorn **between** the peanuts and candy.

He put a quarter on the counter **between** a nickel and a dime, and bought some food.

Bill happily returned to his seat, and sat **between** a bag of popcorn and a bottle of water.

Cut on dotted line

The Perfect Hiding Place

Melanie and Sheila decided to play hide and go seek. First, Melanie went to hide **between** two trees.

Melanie then crawled **between** two bushes, but her feet stuck out.

She tried to hide **between** the fence and the shed, but there were many spider webs.

Finally, Melanie hid in her favorite place. She sat **between** her two brothers on the couch watching T.V.

Cut on dotted line

Kevin the Kangaroo

Kevin the Kangaroo lived at the zoo. He put on **big** tennis shoes and went out for the night.

On the way, he found a **big** floppy hat.

He jumped into a **big** pool to swim with the seals.

Kevin also shared his peanuts with a **big** elephant. What a busy night!

Jerry the Giant

Jerry the Giant lived in a **big** log cabin in the forest.

He likes to eat a **big** stack of pancakes every morning.

After breakfast, he washes his hands with a **big** bar of soap.

Jerry patted his **big** dog, Bart, on the head and left for work with a **big** smile on his face.

2 3
1 4

Cut on dotted line

Bob the Goldfish

Bob the Goldfish liked to blow very **big** bubbles.

When his friends came over, they brought **big** toys with them.

Bob liked to ride in a **big** toy car.

He also liked to blow into the **big** toy tuba.

2 3
1 4

Cut on dotted line

Dominick's Car

Dominick had a problem. His remote-controlled car hit a bump and crashed into a **big** oak tree.

Then it would not stop! It hit a **big** house.

It kept going and ran into a **big** truck!

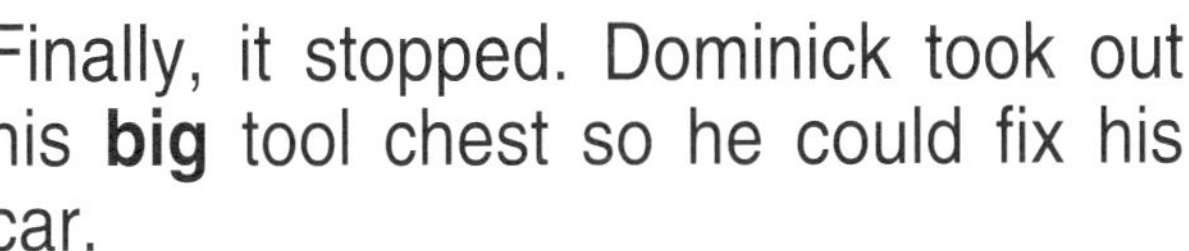

Finally, it stopped. Dominick took out his **big** tool chest so he could fix his car.

Cut on dotted line

Cut on dotted line

Two Terrific Sisters

Brandy and Candy were **both** sisters.

They **both** rode their bikes to school every day.

They **both** loved pizza and salad for lunch.

Every Halloween they **both** dressed up in the same costumes. They were **both** terrific sisters.

Bradley is Silly

Bradley was a silly kid. He loved to wear watches on **both** of his wrists.

He liked to wear **both** of his socks on his hands.

And Bradley liked to wear **both** of his shoes on his hands.

Both of his parents agreed that Bradley was indeed a silly kid.

Cut on dotted line

Sleepy Helena

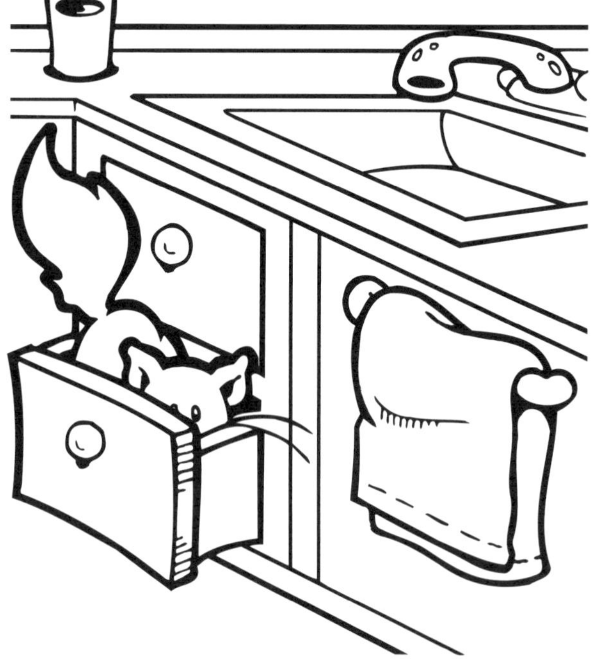

Helena the Cat searched for a comfortable place to sleep. She tried the **bottom** kitchen drawer.

Helena laid down on the **bottom** stair, but people kept tripping over her.

She tried to sleep at the **bottom** of the toy box, but it was too crowded.

The next morning Helena's owners found her sleeping happily in the **bottom** of the bathtub.

Cut on dotted line

Cut on dotted line

Brittany's Glasses

Brittany lost her glasses and couldn't find them anywhere. She looked in the **bottom** of her dresser.

She checked the **bottom** of her closet and still couldn't find them.

She searched the **bottom** of her backpack and there were still no glasses.

When Brittany looked in the **bottom** of the clothes hamper, her glasses slipped off the top of her head!

Cut on dotted line

Shayla's Saxophone

Shayla lived in the **center** of town near the elementary school.

She stood in the **center** of the stage as she tried out for the school band.

Shayla played very well and was put in the **center** of all the saxophone players.

At the school concert, Shayla played a solo under the **center** spotlight.

Cut on dotted line

Tommy's Friends

It was Saturday, and Tommy ran outside. He stood in the **center** of his yard, but nobody was there.

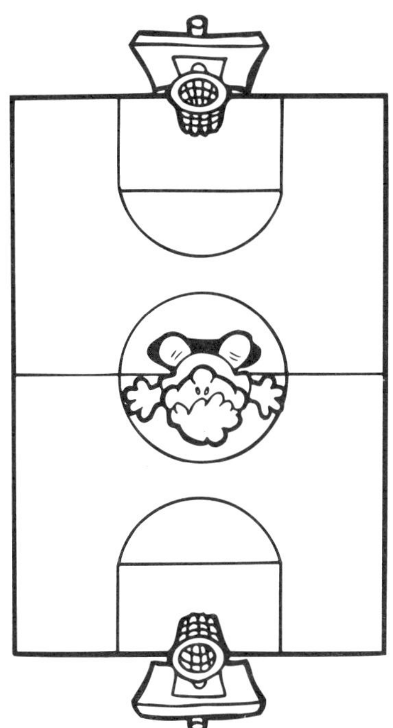

Tommy then ran to the **center** of the basketball court, but it was empty too.

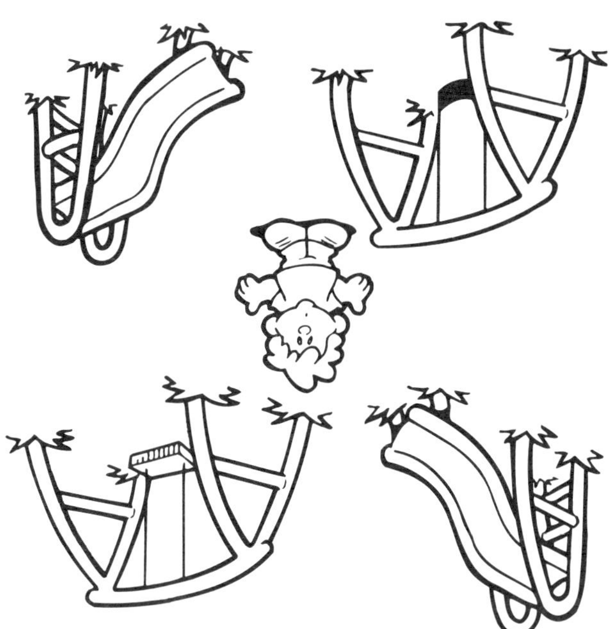

Later, he walked to the **center** of the school playground, but nobody was around. Tommy was sad.

But when he went home, his friends surprised him with a birthday cake in the **center** of his kitchen table.

Barney the Bear

Barney the Bear was getting ready for winter. He put all his fish in the freezer and tried to **close** the door.

He stored his honey jars in a wall safe, and began to **close** it.

Barney would **close** the trunk lid after he pulled out his heavy blankets and pillows.

Tired, Barney got on his bed. Soon his eyes began to **close**. He was ready for his long winter nap.

Raul's Vacation

Raul and his family were going on a vacation. Before they left, Raul's Mom wanted to **close** all the curtains.

Raul had to **close** all the suitcases.

The family walked out of the house, and remembered to **close** the front door.

Raul's Dad put all the luggage in the car trunk. It was hard to **close**!

1 2 3 4

Cut on dotted line

Cut on dotted line

Jose Goes Fishing

Jose and his Dad were going fishing. Jose had to **close** the top of his bag of worms.

Jose's Dad had to **close** the top of the tackle box.

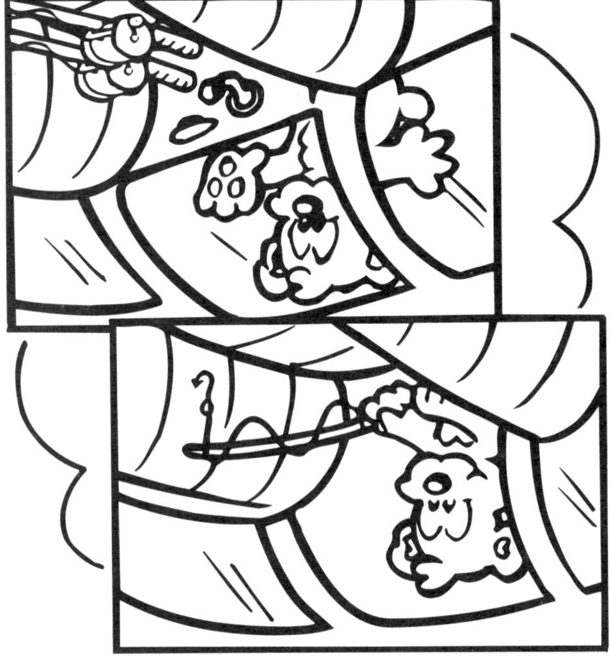

Jose put the fishing poles in the car and then began to **close** the door.

Jose liked to **close** his eyes during the ride to the lake. He dreamed of all the fish he would catch!

Closing the Bakery

Veronica had to **close** the bakery every night. First she would **close** and lock the front door.

Then she would **close** all the store windows.

Next, she would clean out the ovens, and then remember to **close** them.

Finally, she would count all the money and be sure to **close** the cash register.

Andrew's Party

It was the day of Andrew's party. He lived in a two story house on the **corner** of the street.

When Andrew's guests arrived for the party, they were each given three **corner** hats.

A piñata sat on the **corner** of the table waiting to be hung.

All Andrew's friends stood in the **corner** of the room waiting anxiously to hit the piñata.

Monique Counts Corners

Monique was given a homework assignment where she had to count **corners**.

She counted eight **corners** on a cardboard box.

She saw that her tortilla chip has three **corners**.

That evening when she flew her kite, she counted four **corners**. Lots of things have **corners**!

Cut on dotted line

Sherry Wants a Pet

Sherry wanted to pick out a pet of her own. She went to the pet store to look at all the **different** dogs.

Then she went to the Humane Society and saw all the **different** kinds of cats.

Sherry still couldn't decide on a pet. At a bird shop, she saw many **different** birds.

At last, Sherry picked out a pet lizard from many **different** types of reptiles. What an interesting pet!

Cut on dotted line

The Twins Look Different

John and George were twins, but they wore **different** clothes.

George wore a flowered shirt, which was **different** than John's striped shirt.

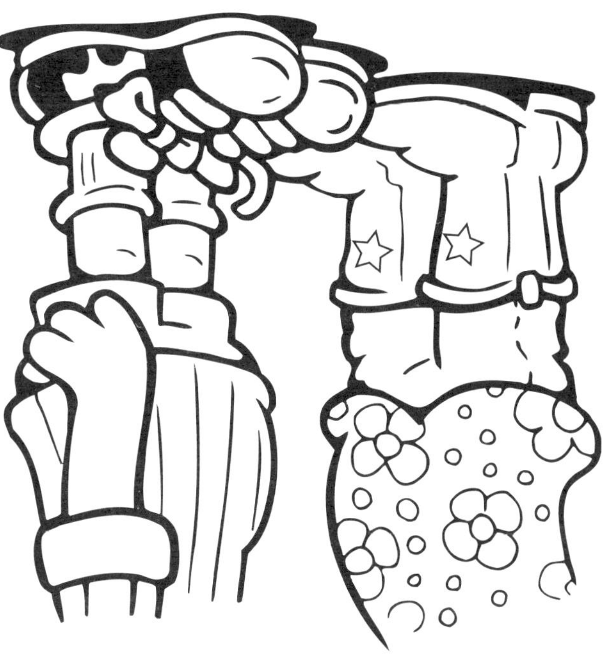

John wore athletic shoes, but George wore something **different** - cowboy boots!

They each wore **different** pants. George wore jeans and John wore shorts.

A Different Day

It was Wacky Wednesday at Lavonna's school. She first put on two **different** socks.

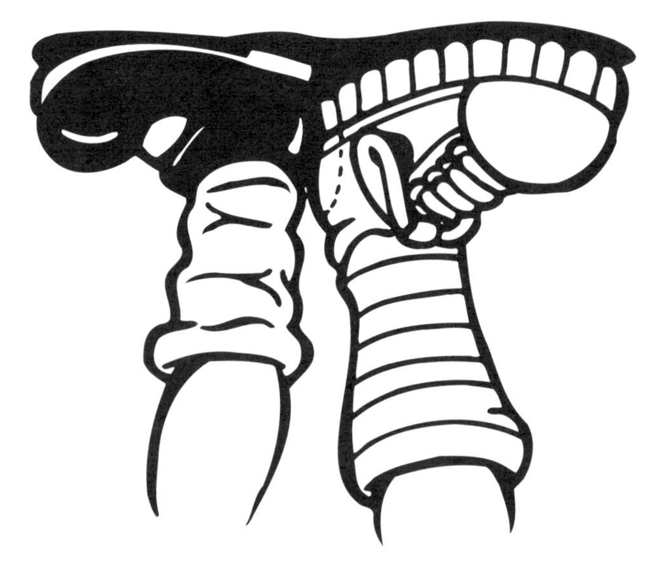

Then she wore two **different** shoes.

She looked in the mirror and decided two **different** earrings would look just great!

Finally. Lavonna added two **different** gloves. She definitely looked **different**!

Cut on dotted line

Cut on dotted line

Micah's parents sat at one table and the children sat at a **different** table.

Tonight they decided to go to a buffet where the family could choose from many **different** foods.

Micah Eats Out

After dinner, Micah had his choice of many **different** desserts. Yum! He decided to try a bite of each one!

Micah and his family eat at a **different** restaurant every Friday night.

Francine Saves Animals

Francine Firefighter ran **down** the stairs and jumped on the fire engine.

The first stop was to save Fifi the French poodle. Fifi had accidentally fallen **down** a well.

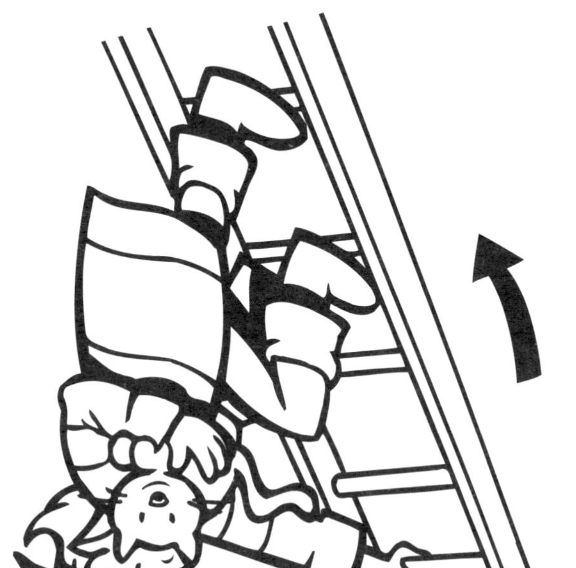

Francine carefully rescued Curly the Cat and climbed safely **down** the ladder.

When Francine returned to the fire station, she stepped **down** from the fire engine. Great work, Francine!

Cut on dotted line

Cut on dotted line

Lizanne's Amusing Day

At the amusement park, Lizanne rode **down** a fast roller coaster ride.

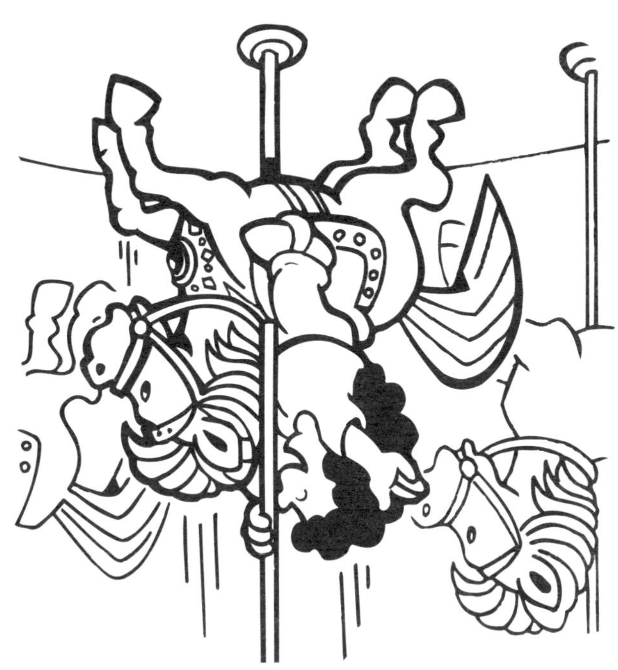

Next, she went on the merry-go-round. Lizanne rode on a horse that gently went up and **down**.

It got hot, so Lizanne went **down** the twisty water slides to cool off.

Lizanne was hungry, so she walked **down** the hill to buy a giant ice cream cone.

Going Down the Hill

Jacob and Josh wanted to go **down** a hill where they lived.

Jacob rode **down** on his bike.

Josh rode **down** on his skateboard.

Their mother drove **down** the hill in her van! Who do you think got **down** the hill first?

1 2 3 4

Cut on dotted line

Shopping Downtown

Gary loved going to the mall with his dad because he could ride **down** the escalators.

He also loved pushing the buttons to ride **down** on the elevators.

Gary and his Dad walked **down** the stairs to see other shops and restaurants.

When Gary and his Dad were done shopping, they went **down** into the parking garage to get their car.

Cut on dotted line

Greg the Gorilla

Greg the Gorilla loved to eat. His plate of bananas was soon **empty**.

The zookeeper gave him a pineapple in a bowl. Soon, the bowl was **empty**.

The zookeeper gave Greg a thick milkshake. The glass was **empty** almost immediately.

The zookeeper said, “Greg, you need to exercise!” Greg’s cage was **empty** while he took a walk.

Bonnie Loves Camping

Bonnie Bear loved to roam the camp and look for **empty** campsites.

She was disappointed when she found **empty** garbage cans.

If she were lucky, she might find a cooler to **empty** out.

When Bonnie entered the camper's tent, it would be **empty** in no time!

Cut on dotted line

The Birthday Present

Cassie wanted to buy her Dad a birthday present. She shook her piggy bank, but it was **empty**.

She checked her wallet and it was **empty** too.

She looked in all of her coat pockets and found them **empty** as well.

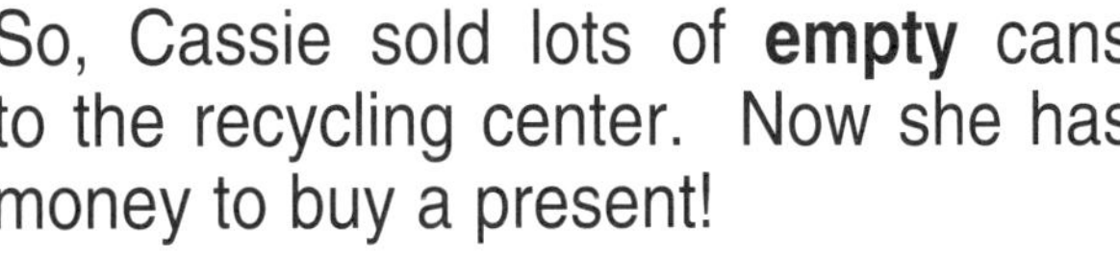

So, Cassie sold lots of **empty** cans to the recycling center. Now she has money to buy a present!

Cut on dotted line

Janitor Joe

Janitor Joe came to work when all the classrooms were **empty**.

First, he threw out the trash from the wastepaper baskets so they were **empty**.

Next, he cleaned out the pencil sharpener, so it was **empty** too.

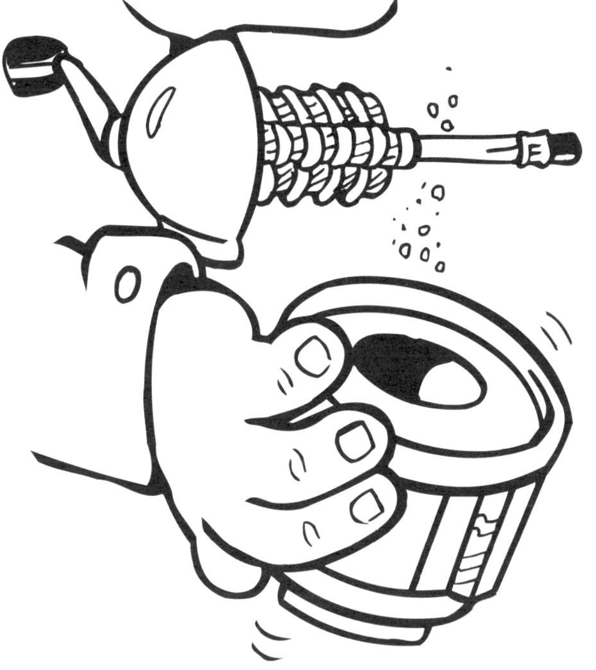

When he finished mopping, he threw out the dirty water and put the **empty** mop bucket on the shelf.

Cut on dotted line

Going to the Movies

Victor wanted to go to the movie theater. It was located at the **end** of the street.

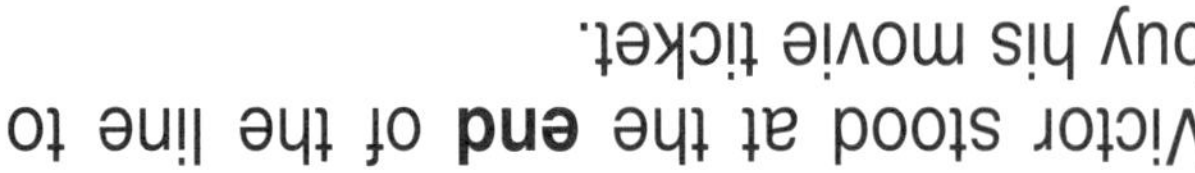
Victor stood at the **end** of the line to buy his movie ticket.

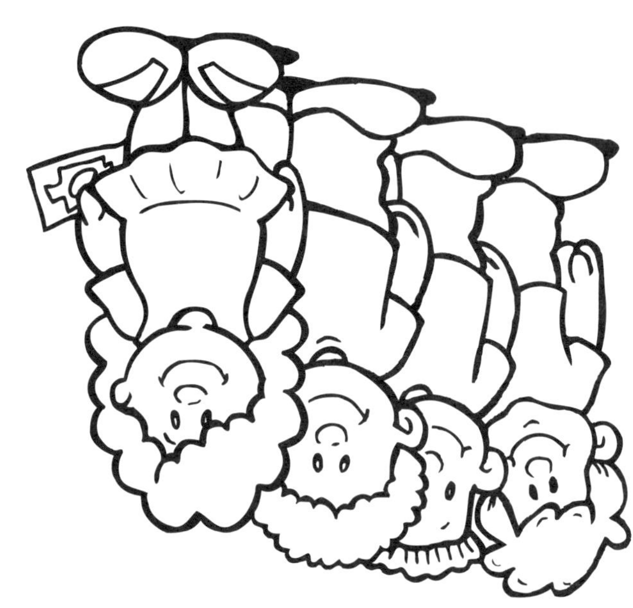

He walked into the theater and sat at the **end** of the row.

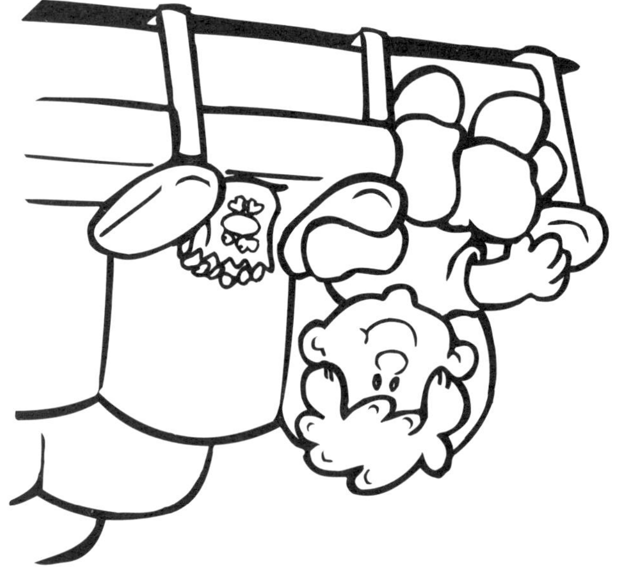

The movie was very funny. He laughed and laughed until "The **End**" appeared on the screen.

Cut on dotted line

Tammy at the Pool

Tammy went to the pool for the day. She parked her bicycle at the **end** of the bike rack.

Then she sat down and read a magazine from beginning to **end**.

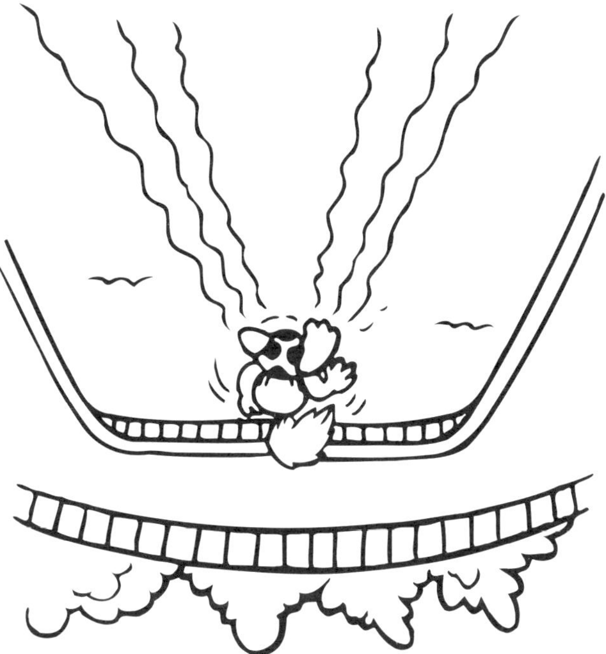

When she became hot, Tammy jumped into the water and swam to the **end** of the pool.

Then, she returned to her chair and dried the **end** of her hair with a towel.

1 2 3 4

Ronnie Robot

Ronnie Robot cooked breakfast **every** day for his family.

For breakfast, Ronnie cooked enough pancakes so **every** person could eat four.

After breakfast, he cleaned **every** plate until each one sparkled.

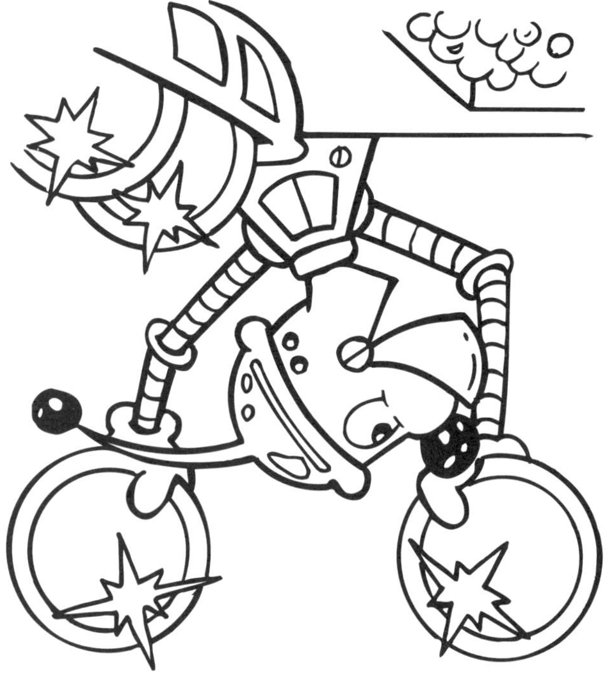

Every member of Ronnie's family said, "thank you," for all of his help.

Cut on dotted line

Leanne has a Birthday

Leanne liked to eat **every** food her Mom put in her lunchbox.

She also drank **every** drink her Mom packed.

For her birthday, Leanne brought chocolate cupcakes for **every** student in her class.

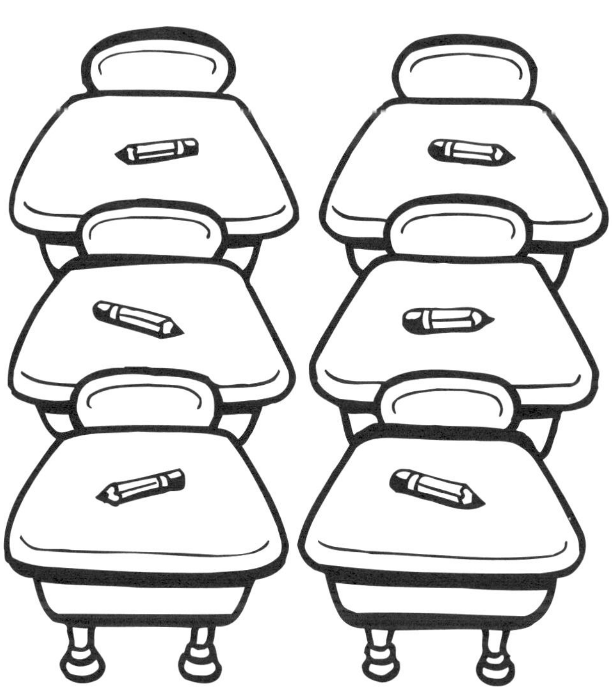

She also put a birthday pencil on **every** desk. Leanne wished **every** day was her birthday.

Cut on dotted line

Sammy Lives Far Away

Sammy the Seal lived on a rock **far** from shore. He was a silly seal that loved to polka dance.

Tourists flew in from **far, far,** away to take pictures of Sammy dancing the polka.

One sad day, Sammy caught the chicken pox and he had to stay **far** away from the other seals.

But even **far** away, every one watched polka dotted Sammy dance the polka.

Cut on dotted line

Looking Far Away

Chester loved to look out his window at the buildings and mountains **far** from his house.

His parents bought him a telescope so he could look into the sky and see **far** away stars.

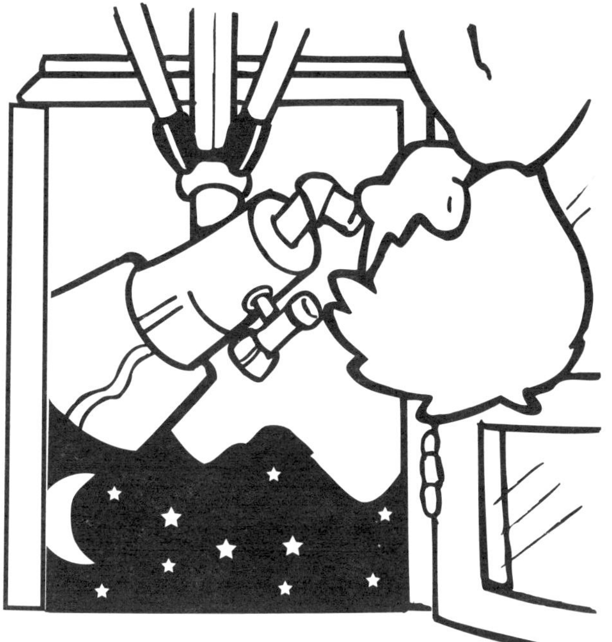

The first time Chester used his telescope, he could see the moon **far** away too.

When he slept, he dreamed of visiting **far** away planets.

Tony the Tortoise

Tony the Tortoise lifted weights **fast** so he could become stronger.

Soon, Tony could walk **fast**.

He could also skip **fast**.

At the animal race he ran so **fast** he won the race! Yes, Tony was one **fast** tortoise!

3 2
4 1

Cut on dotted line

Cut on dotted line

Nikki is Fast

Nikki loved to do everything **fast**. She climbed trees **fast**.

She swam in the pool **fast**.

She even read books **fast**.

Nikki was one **fast** girl! After a busy day, she would fall asleep **fast** on her bed.

Cut on dotted line

Sandy Thinks Fast

Sandy saw the house across the street catch on fire. She ran **fast** to call for help.

The fire engines drove **fast** to the house.

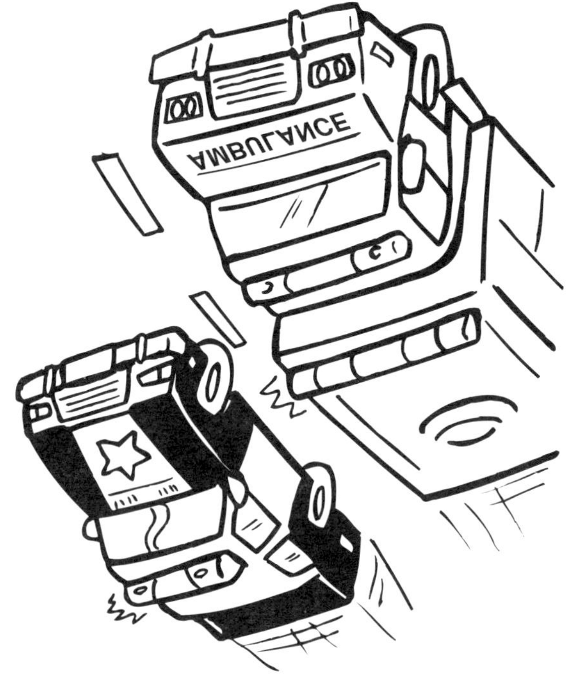

The police officers and ambulance drivers drove **fast** too!

Using their hoses, the firefighters worked **fast** and saved the house. **Fast** thinking Sandy!

www.superduperinc.com • 1-800-277-8737

Cut on dotted line

Wendy the Whale

Wendy the Whale swam **fast** in the ocean. She liked to swim with her friends.

Suzie the Seagull flew **fast** above Wendy.

Shayla the Shark swam **fast** beside Wendy.

How did they all swim so **fast**? Every day they took their vitamins and ate healthy food.

Cut on dotted line

Mary the Mouse

Mary the Mouse had a **few** friends over to her mouse hole.

She put a **few** slices of cheese on a plate and offered it to her guests.

Mary then put a **few** chips on the table and offered juice to her friends.

The doorbell rang and a **few** more friends arrived. It turned into quite a party!

1 2 3 4

www.superduperinc.com • 1-800-277-8737

Drawing Fun

Howard wanted to enter a drawing contest. He found a **few** pieces of paper he could draw on.

He picked up a **few** pencils with erasers to use for sketching and shading.

He also grabbed a **few** colored markers.

Then, Howard made a **few** drawings. He had lots of fun!

Arnie is First

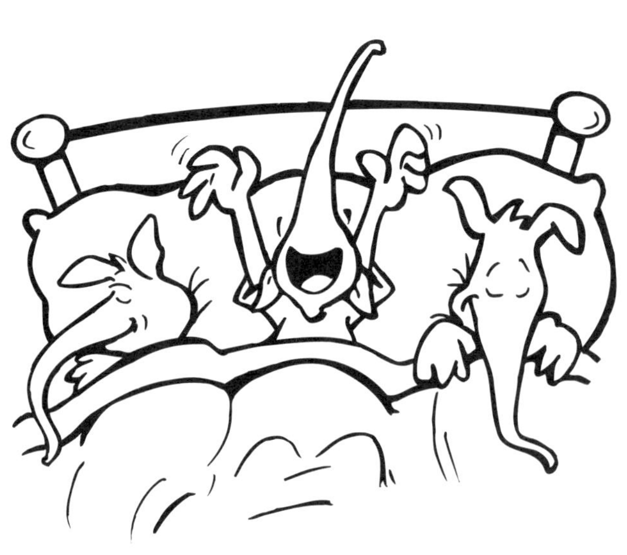

Arnie the Anteater was the **first** one to wake up in his family.

He headed to the kitchen cupboards and took a bowl from the **first** shelf.

He was the **first** one to sit down at the table for breakfast.

Soon, his Mom came down and gave gave him the **first** kiss of the day.

Cut on dotted line

First Day of School

It was the **first** day of school for Desiree Aardvark.

She was in the **first** grade.

She sat at the **first** desk.

She was also **first** in line for lunch. Why was Desiree always **first**?

Jolene the Painter

Jolene was a wonderful painter. She often painted pictures of dogs and cats on the **front** of pet stores.

She painted a beautiful rainbow on the **front** of a nearby school.

At parties, children loved to have Jolene paint the **front** of their T-shirts.

She even painted a picture on the **front** of her car! Jolene was one talented painter!

Cut on dotted line

Cut on dotted line

The Snowman

Bruce looked out his **front** window and saw it was snowing.

He put on his warm clothes and ran out the **front** door.

He built a terrific looking snowman on his **front** lawn for everyone to see.

Bruce hung a note on the **front** of the snowman that said, "Hug a snowman today!"

Halloween House

Every Halloween, Hans loved to decorate the **front** of his house.

He placed a witch with a broom on the **front** porch.

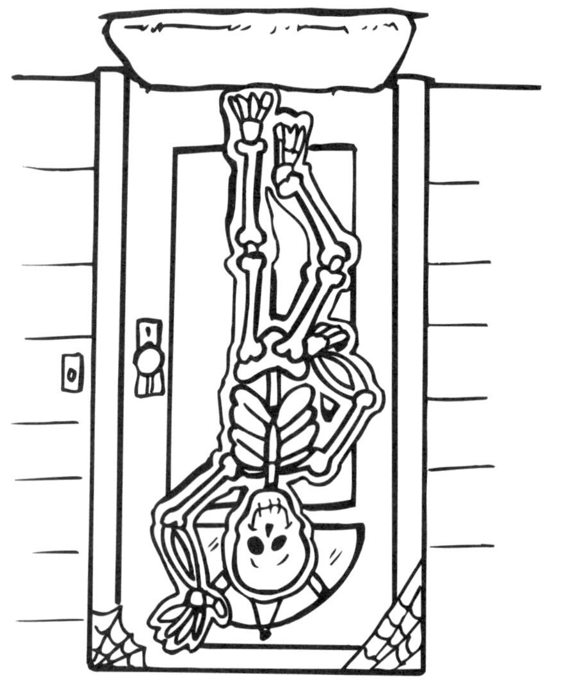

On the **front** door, he put up a friendly skeleton.

Hans built a big scarecrow in **front** of his bushes. Everyone agreed that Hans' house looked terrific!

Cut on dotted line

Cut on dotted line

Sharing with Friends

Radine the Rooster baked two apple pies and put them in **front** of a fan so they would cool off.

Her friends Cherry Chicken and Terry Turkey sat down in **front** of the pies.

Then, Radine put a delicious slice of pie in **front** of each of them.

Terry Turkey was a messy eater. He dribbled pie on the **front** of his shirt.

Special Presents

Chelsea loved to make special presents, like a basket **full** of chocolate candies.

For her Mom, she arranged a vase **full** of her favorite flowers.

Chelsea made her Dad a tool box **full** of his favorite things — nails, screws, and small tools.

Chelsea gave her neighbors boxes **full** of brownies, cupcakes, and candies.

Cut on dotted line

Cut on dotted line

Everything is Full

Hannah received a box **full** of cookies.

She wanted to put the cookies in the pantry, but it was **full**.

She tried to put them in the refrigerator, but it was **full** too!

Hannah decided to walk around with a box **full** of cookies to share with everyone!

A Full House

Logan decided to visit his grandma for Christmas. He packed his suitcase **full** of clothes.

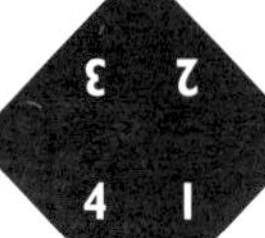

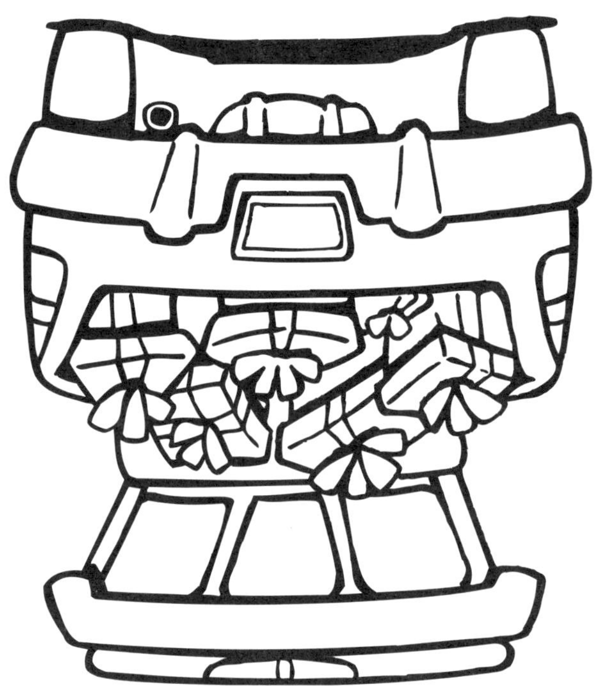

The trunk of his car was **full** of presents!

When he arrived, his grandmother's house was **full** of friends and relatives.

Even the Christmas tree was **full** of ornaments. Everyone had a wonderful time!

Cut on dotted line

Cut on dotted line

Day at the Beach

Charles was going to the beach. He filled his ice chest **full** of sodas and bottled water.

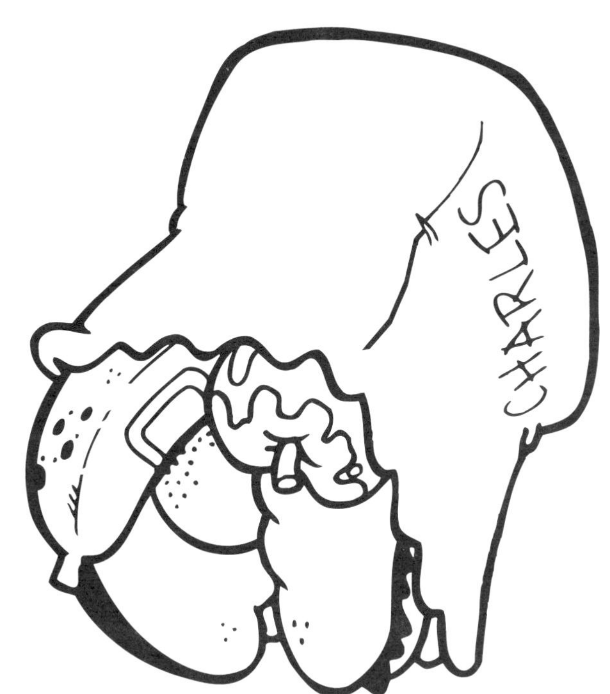

His Mom knew he would get hungry, so she packed Charles a sack **full** of sandwiches and fruit.

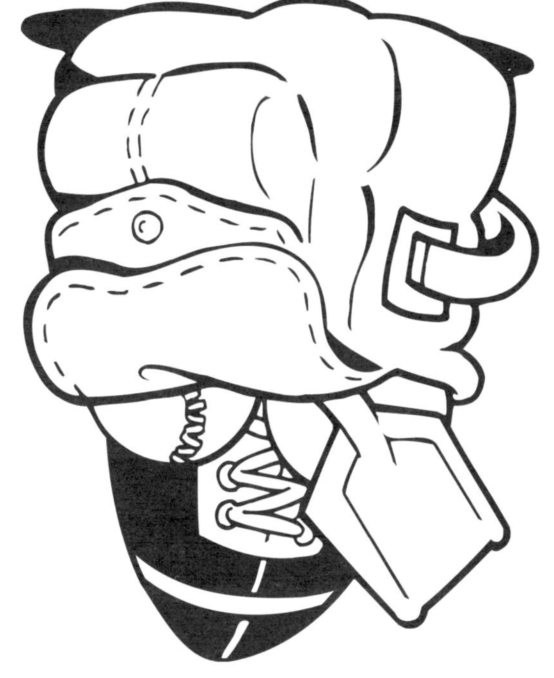

Charles made sure his backpack was **full** of sports equipment and toys.

After spending all day at the beach, Charles came home with shoes **full** of sand.

Dean Eats Half

Dean loved to eat **half** of his meals. For breakfast he ate **half** a pancake.

For lunch, he ate **half** a sandwich, **half** of his apple, and **half** of a cookie.

Dean even drank **half** of his glass of milk.

Luckily for Dean, his sister ate the other **half** of his food. That way, no food was wasted!

Cut on dotted line

Madison Does Half

Madison only did **half** of her chores. She mowed only **half** of the lawn.

She vacuumed and cleaned only **half** her room.

After school, she finished only **half** of her homework.

To teach her a lesson, Madison's parents gave her **half** of a hamburger with **half** a soda for dinner.

Cut on dotted line

Andre the Strong Ant

Andre the Ant loved to carry **heavy** things. He lifted a **heavy** grapefruit above his head.

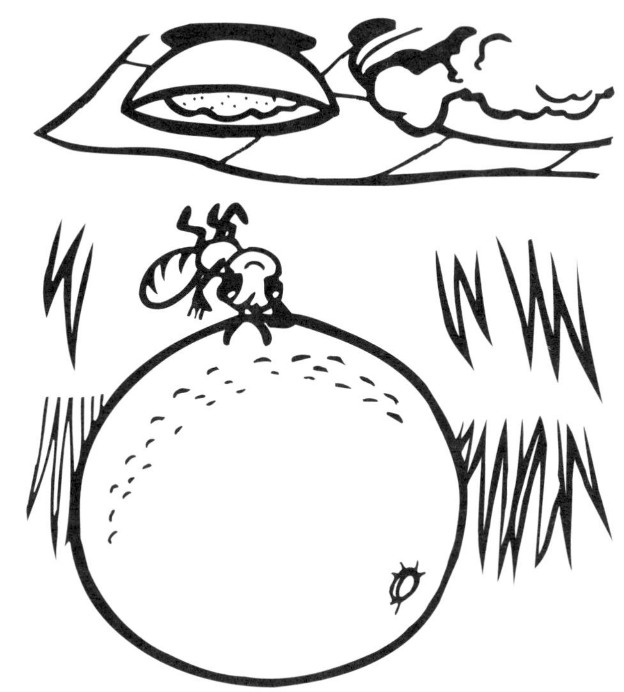

For the summer picnic, Andre brought a **heavy** cantaloupe all by himself.

For his friend's birthday party, Andre carried in a **heavy** chocolate cake with four candles.

Andre was strong, but Andrea was stronger. She could lift a **heavy** watermelon.

2 3
4 1

Cut on dotted line

Cut on dotted line

Trixie the Truck

Trixie the Truck carried **heavy** loads all around town.

She hauled **heavy** bricks to construction workers who were building houses.

She unloaded **heavy** sand piles at the playgrounds and parks.

Trixie even carried **heavy** refrigerators to restaurants. Trixie was very helpful!

Perry the Heavyweight

Perry the Penguin lifted **heavy** weights at the gym.

He was so strong he could lift three **heavy** fish using just his beak.

Perry even lifted **heavy** blocks of ice above his head.

He won the "Strongest Penguin" contest and lifted the **heavy** trophy above his head.

Cut on dotted line

Cut on dotted line

Visiting Grandma

Romero carried some **heavy** suitcases to the car. His family was going to visit grandma.

He also carried a **heavy** cooler filled with bottled water.

He dragged a **heavy** bag full of toys and games.

But when all these things were on the car, it was too **heavy** to move. What do you think Romero did next?

Eric Takes Pictures

Eric bought a new camera. First, he took a picture of a hiker climbing a **high** mountain.

He then snapped a picture of his best friend jumping over some **high** hurdles.

When Eric saw a helicopter **high** in the sky, he took a picture of it.

Last, Eric took a picture of his sister climbing **high** up a tree. Eric loved taking pictures!

2 3
1 4

Cut on dotted line

High Flying Carpet

A wizard gave Jasmine a magic carpet. She flew **high** over the houses.

She flew **high** above the trees in the forest.

She flew **high** above the city skyscrapers.

Jasmine flew so **high** she could touch the clouds! Jasmine even waved at **high** flying birds.

Cut on dotted line

On the way home, he stood **in** a mud puddle.

When he got home, his Mom said, "take off those muddy boots and put them **in** the garage!"

3 2

4 1

Tommy in the Puddle

It was raining, so Tommy put his books **in** his backpack to keep them dry.

Tommy was all muddy, so he had to get **in** the bathtub and scrub, scrub, scrub!

Cut on dotted line

Video Games

Jeff and Brian were stuck **in** the house because it was a rainy day.

They loved to play video games **in** their bedroom.

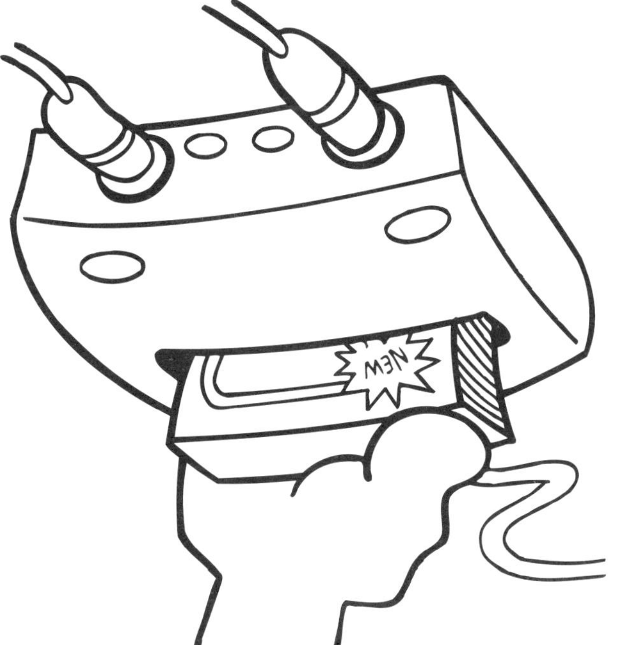

They put their favorite game **in** the machine and began to play. The boys played all day.

That night, Jeff and Brian fell asleep with the controls still **in** their hands.

Jessica's Vase

Jessica wanted to give her mother something special. She bought a vase and carried it home **in** a bag.

First, she put water **in** the vase.

Then, Jessica put roses and ferns **in** the vase.

Her Mom loved the vase and held it **in** her hands. Wasn't Jessica a very thoughtful girl?

Cut on dotted line

Bunny's Halloween

On Halloween night, Stacy put on her costume **in** her room.

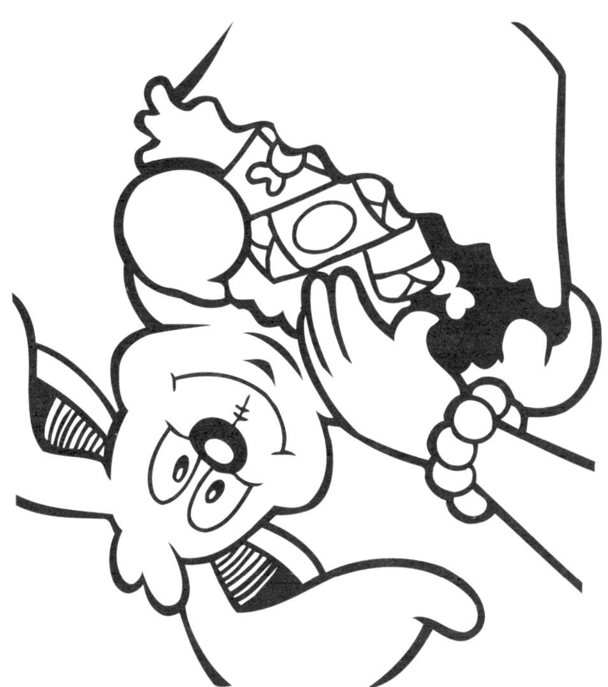

After she dressed, her mother took her to the neighbor's house. Her friend put candy **in** her bag.

Next, Stacy and her Mom went to the farmhouse. The farmer put a bunch of carrots **in** her bag!

When Stacy got home, she put some of the carrots **in** her rabbit's dish. Happy Halloween, Bunny!

Kindergarten

On the first day of school, the teachers parked their cars **in a row** facing the school.

Mrs. Weinstock, the kindergarten teacher, made sure the desks in her room were placed neatly **in a row**.

She organized the bookcase and put all the reading books **in a row**.

The students even lined up **in a row** in front of her classroom. She knew it would be a great year!

Cut on dotted line

#BK-278 Fold & Say® Basic Concept Stories ©1999 Super Duper® Publications
www.superduperinc.com • 1-800-277-8737

Cut on dotted line

Ethan's Surprise

Ethan wanted to surprise his Mom by cleaning up the house. He put the cereal boxes neatly **in a row**.

He organized his sister's room by putting all her stuffed animals **in a row** on a shelf.

He picked up his toy soldiers off the floor and put them **in a row** on his dresser.

His Mom loved flowers, so he planted five daisies **in a row** in the yard. Ethan's Mom loved them!

Going to a Concert

Maureen drove **in front of** the stadium to see her favorite group, the Groovy Gourds.

She parked her bike and then walked **in front of** the ticket booth to buy a ticket.

She lined up **in front of** the gate before going into the stadium.

She had a great seat **in front of** the band. She took lots of pictures to show all of her friends.

2 3
1 4

Cut on dotted line

1 2 3 4

Going for Ice Cream

Matt and Lindsay stood **in front of** the ice cream shop.

They went in and sat down **in front of** the counter.

They looked at the menu the waitress put **in front of** them. They ordered their favorite dessert.

Before they knew it, the most delicious ice cream sundae was put **in front of** them.

The Ball

Princess Patti stood **in front of** the mirror. It was the night of the grand ball.

Several of the king's men decorated the castle by putting up lights **in front of** the towers.

Later that evening, people lined up **in front of** the castle to greet the king and his family.

When all the guests were inside, everyone danced **in front of** the band. It was a wonderful party!

Cut on dotted line

Going to the Movies

Joe stood **in front of** his mom at the ticket counter. He was going to see a monster movie.

He ran to the snack bar and stood **in front of** many people. He ordered buttered popcorn.

Joe sat in the first row **in front of** all the other people.

When the movie started, Joe saw a friendly monster right **in front of** him. What a great movie!

Things in Order

Denny the Dog liked everything to be **in order**. His dog bones were **in order** from to smallest to biggest .

His leashes were **in order** from shortest to longest.

Even Denny's dog food cans were put **in order** by flavor.

Denny was so organized that he arranged his toys **in order** too.

Cut on dotted line

Cut on dotted line

Devon's Chores

Devon's Mom gave her a list of chores to do. First, she put her vacation pictures **in order.**

Then she baked chocolate chip cookies. She was careful to add the ingredients **in order.**

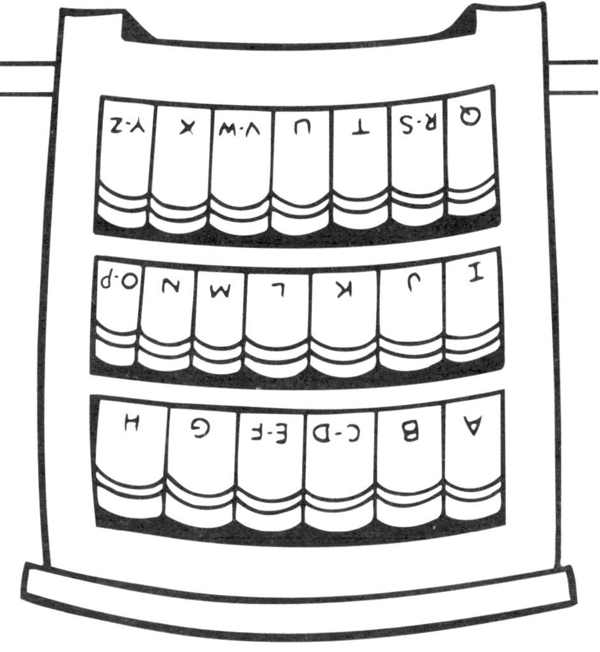

Next, she arranged the books on the bookshelf **in order** from A to Z.

Last, she cleaned up the garage by putting all the rakes, shovels, and brooms **in order**. Good job!

2 3
1 4

Ready for School

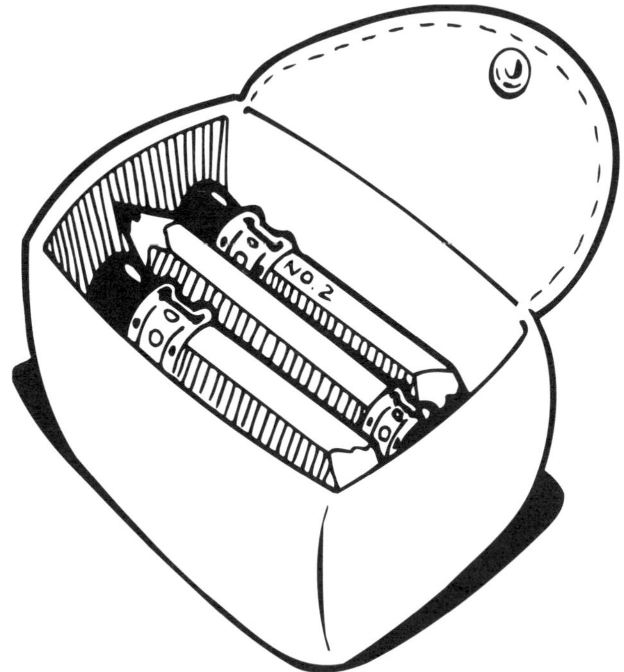

Tanisha was getting ready for school. She put her pencils **inside** her pencil pouch.

She placed her books and homework **inside** her backpack.

Tanisha opened her lunch box and put a sandwich, apple, and drink **inside** it.

Tanisha ran out to the garage and jumped **inside** the car. She was ready for school!

Cut on dotted line

Cut on dotted line

Going to the Pet Store

Roger went to the pet store to look at all the animals. He first saw a big parrot **inside** a cage.

He walked down the aisle and saw lots of fish swimming **inside** the aquarium.

Roger spotted three puppies lying **inside** a great big doghouse.

Finally, Roger watched the turtles **inside** the terrarium eating their vegetables. Roger loved pets!

An Unusual Day

Collin was having an unusual day. He got the **last** pancake at breakfast.

He was the **last** one in line at the bus stop.

Collin was **last** in line to buy lunch.

When his family went to the movies that night, they had to sit in the **last** row. How unusual!

1 2 3 4

Cut on dotted line

Alex Was Last

Alex the Alligator was always the **last** one at everything. He was the **last** one to get into the river.

He was the **last** one to dry off after his swim.

Alex was the **last** one to get an afternoon snack.

Alex was even the **last** one to go to bed at night. “Good night, Alex.”

The Twins

Jean and Janice are twins. Jean has the **least** number of freckles on her face.

Janice has the **least** number of dots on her shirt.

Jean wears the **least** number of rings on her fingers.

Janice has the **least** number of books, but they both love to read.

1 2 3 4

Cut on dotted line

Dimitri Shops

Dimitri went grocery shopping. He picked the basket with the **least** strawberries.

He needed a watermelon, so he picked the one that weighed the **least**.

Dimitri picked a donut with the **least** number of sprinkles on top.

He stood at the checkout line with the **least** amount of other shoppers.

Lefty Luke

Luke did everything with the **left** side of his body. He wrote with his **left** hand.

He kicked the soccer ball with his **left** foot.

He threw the ball using his **left** hand.

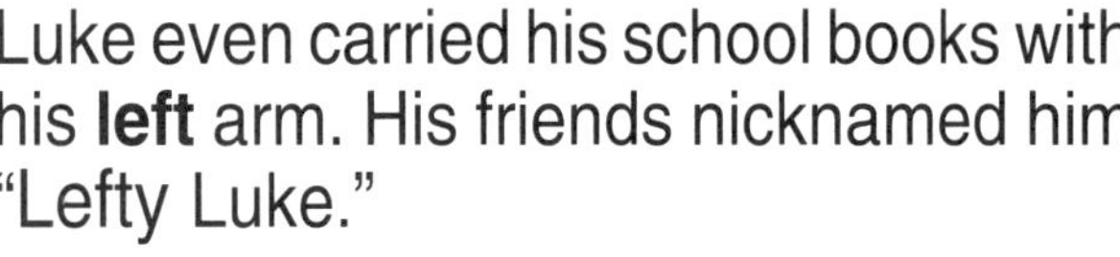

Luke even carried his school books with his **left** arm. His friends nicknamed him "Lefty Luke."

Cut on dotted line

Darren Dresses Up

It was dress up day at Darren's school. He wore a silly shoe on his **left** foot.

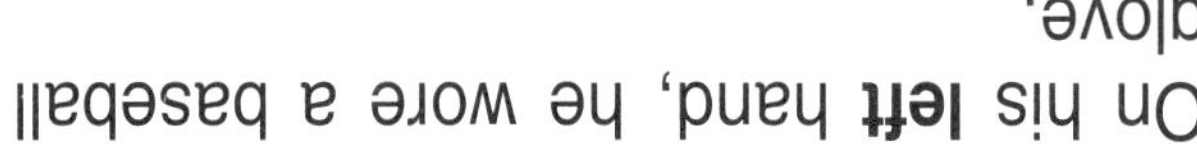

On his **left** hand, he wore a baseball glove.

Darren put a stuffed owl on his **left** shoulder.

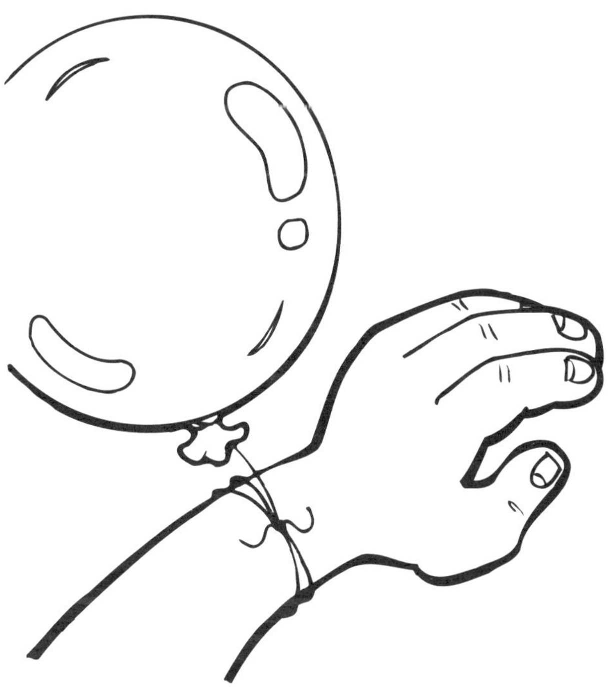

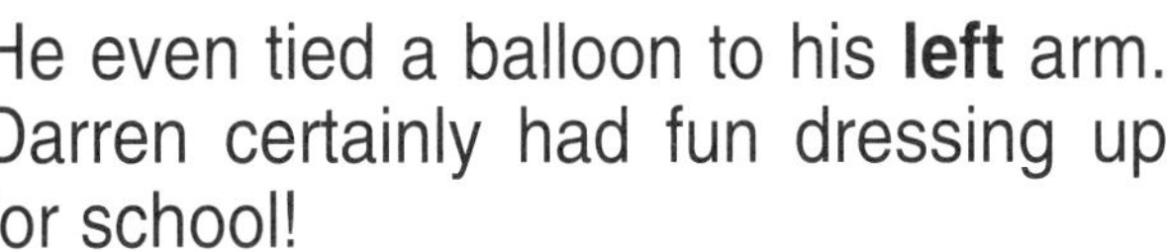

He even tied a balloon to his **left** arm. Darren certainly had fun dressing up for school!

Cut on dotted line

Bailey Bear

Bailey was a little bear. She ate **less** than the other bears in her family.

She drank **less** than her big brother Brad.

She carried **less** dishes to the sink than her Dad.

She put away **less** dishes than her Mom. But, Bailey always did her best!

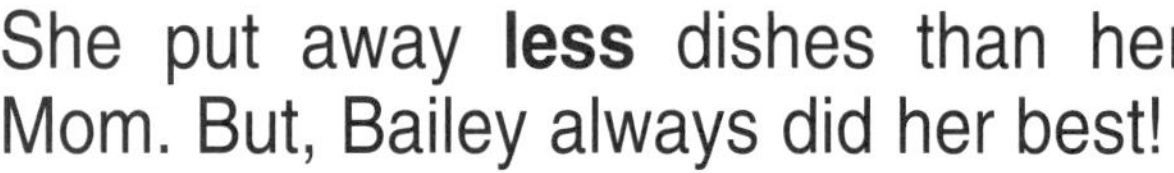

Cut on dotted line

Cut on dotted line

Two Sisters

Donna and Heather were sisters. They shared a bedroom. Donna had **less** toys than Heather.

Donna had **less** books than Heather on their bookshelf.

Donna had **less** shoes than her sister in their closet.

Donna also had **less** stuffed animals on her bed than Heather.

Mona Packs Light

Mona wanted her suitcase to be as **light** as possible. So, she packed **light** shorts rather than her heavy pants.

She took her **light** raincoat rather than her heavy winter coat.

Mona put in her **light** T-shirt instead of her bulky sweater.

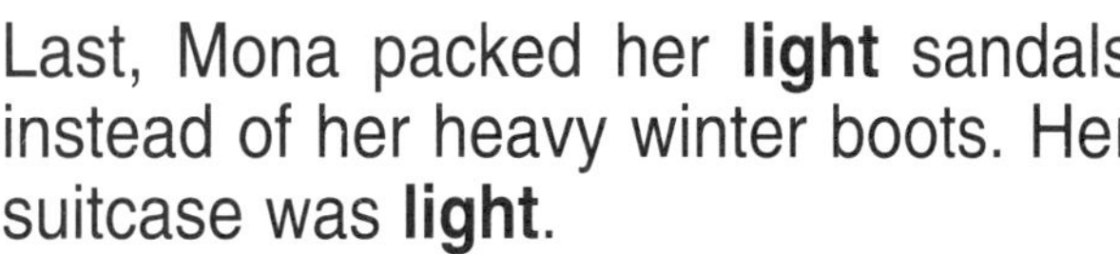

Last, Mona packed her **light** sandals instead of her heavy winter boots. Her suitcase was **light**.

2 3
1 4

Cut on dotted line

A Science Experiment

Doug's class did an experiment using scales. A pencil was **light**, and a book was heavy.

The paper clip was **light** and the stapler was heavy.

The dime was **light** and the paperweight was heavy.

The last experiment showed an eraser was **light** and Doug's full lunch box was heavy.

1 2 3 4

Cut on dotted line

Chrissy's Little Room

In Chrissy's room, all the **little** stuffed animals came for a tea party.

The stuffed bears brought three **little** cakes.

The **little** puppies came in with lots of **little** bone shaped cookies.

The **little** bunnies brought a teapot with lots of **little** cups and saucers. What a great party!

3 2
4 1

Cut on dotted line

Cut on dotted line

Lacey the Ladybug

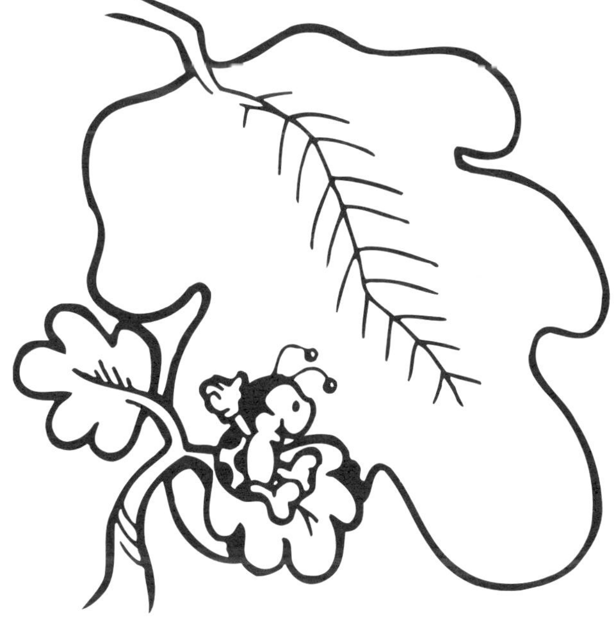

Lacey was a **little** ladybug who lived on a **little** leaf.

Lacy loved to fly around town with her friend, **little** Emma the mosquito.

On sunny days Lacey wore a **little** pair of sunglasses and a **little** bikini.

Lacey and Emma liked to go to the beach and buy **little** beach towels.

Little Liz

Liz was a **little** lion. She liked to go on long walks.

One day, Liz found a **little** frog caught under a branch.

Liz used her **little** paw to move the branch and set the **little** frog free.

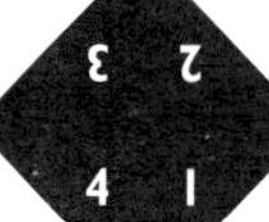

The **little** frog thanked Liz and gave her a **little** whistle. “Blow the whistle and I’ll come play with you!” he said.

Cut on dotted line

Cut on dotted line

A Lucky Little Ant

Tony was a **little** ant who lived close to a river.

Everyday Tony took his **little** raft and floated across the river to a park.

He then pulled his **little** raft out of the river and looked for **little** crumbs of bread and fruit.

Sometimes, lucky Tony found a **little** ice cream. Tony really liked ice cream!

Evan and Bobo

Evan saw it was snowing outside. He put on his **long** pants.

Next, he put on a **long** coat.

Evan added a **long** scarf and cap to keep him warm.

Then Evan put a **long** leash on his dog Bobo. They went for a **long** winter walk around the block.

Cut on dotted line

Cut on dotted line

Going to the Ballet

Nancy was excited to go to the ballet with her family. She put on her **long** skirt.

The family had to stand in a **long** line before getting into the auditorium.

Nancy bought a **long** licorice stick to snack on during intermission.

Nancy saw the ballerinas get into their **long** limousine at the end of the ballet.

2 3
1 4

They came to a fence and crawled **low** to get under it.

They saw a bee buzzing **low** near a flower.

2 3
1 4

Going on a Walk

Shem and Tatiana went on a long walk. They saw a toy airplane flying **low** near the ground.

Then they laid **low** under a shady tree and took a nap.

Cut on dotted line

Cut on dotted line

A Trip to the River

Paul wanted to go to the river. He took out his binoculars from a **low** shelf in his closet.

When he arrived at the river, Paul looked through his binoculars and saw a bird flying **low** near the water.

Paul looked down to see a snake slithering **low** in the grass.

He walked quickly away from the river. Paul was careful to not hit his head on the **low** branches.

Cut on dotted line

Too Many Things

Roy had too **many** things in his bedroom.

In his desk drawer, he found **many** pencils and erasers.

On his bookshelf, he counted **many** comic books and baseball cards.

Even his toy box had too **many** toys. Roy decided to give some of his toys to his baby brother.

3 2
4 1

Cut on dotted line

Camille is So Silly

Camille was a silly girl. She wore **many** bracelets around her wrists.

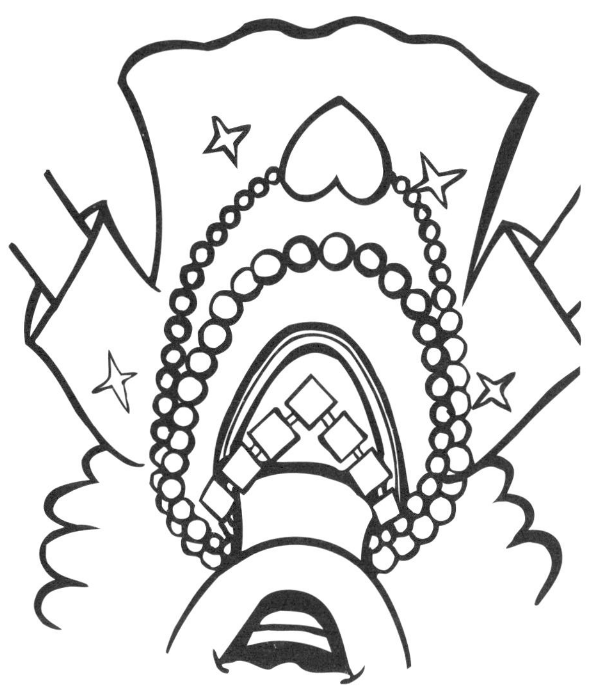

She put **many** necklaces around her neck.

Camille put **many** hats on her head.

She even wore too **many** socks on her feet. Camille couldn't move with everything she wore!

Alvin's Midday Snack

Alvin sat in the **middle** of his bed and heard his stomach growling.

He was hungry. So, he took two pieces of bread and put a piece of cheese in the **middle**.

He put butter in the **middle** of the frying pan and fried the sandwich.

Alvin placed the grilled cheese sandwich in the **middle** of his plate. It smelled great!

1 2 3 4

Cut on dotted line

Cut on dotted line

Holly's Happy Birthday

Holly stood in the **middle** of the room as everyone sang "Happy Birthday" to her.

There was a great big candle in the **middle** of Holly's birthday cake.

Holly's Mom put the cake in the **middle** of the kitchen table.

Holly sat in the **middle** of the couch opening all her presents. It was a wonderful birthday!

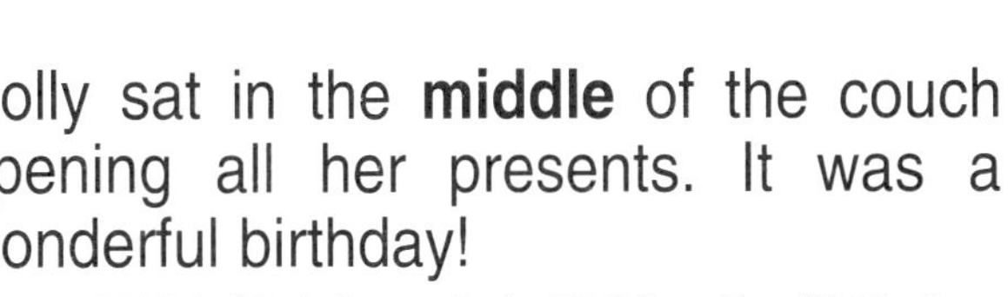

Cut on dotted line

Betsy Beaver

Betsy Beaver was a busy beaver. She cut **more** wood than any of her beaver friends.

She stacked **more** wood than her beaver buddies.

Betsy stored **more** food under her beaver dam than the other beavers.

Betsy also had **more** beaver babies than any beaver in town. That's what kept her so busy!

Cut on dotted line

Duke Wants More!

Deena asked her Mom for a glass of milk. Duke wanted **more** milk and asked for two glasses.

Deena took one hamburger. Duke wanted **more** and took two hamburgers.

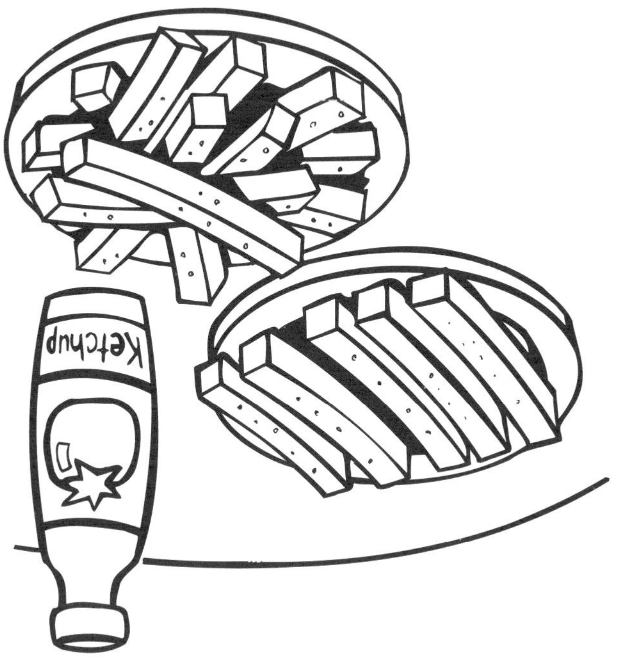

When it came to the fries, Deena put five french fries on her plate. Duke had **more** on his plate!

For dessert, Deena had one scoop of vanilla ice cream. Duke had **more** scoops. Yum, yum!

2 3
1 4

Race Car Drivers

Ricky Racer, Lightning Larry, and Speedy Sally were race car drivers. Ricky had won the **most** medals.

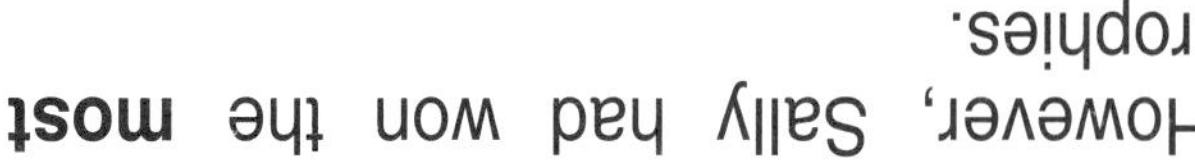

However, Sally had won the **most** trophies.

Larry had the **most** stickers on his car.

After each race, Ricky drank the **most** water to cool off. But, they all were winners!

1 2 3 4

Cut on dotted line

#BK-278 Fold & Say® Basic Concept Stories ©1999 Super Duper® Publications
www.superduperinc.com • 1-800-277-8737

Cut on dotted line

Marci, Mark, and Mindy

Marci, Mark, and Mindy counted the money in their piggy banks. Marci had the **most** money.

They all wore neat clothes. Mark's pants had the **most** pockets.

Mindy's shirt had the **most** buttons.

Marci's hat had the **most** flowers on it.

Princess Penny

Princess Penny loved to go into the forest **near** her castle.

She liked to walk **near** the winding creek.

Princess Penny brought food and scattered it on the ground **near** her feet.

The animals raced to get **near** her so they could eat the food.

Cut on dotted line

Cut on dotted line

Christmas Surprise

On Christmas eve, Tanya left a plate of cookies with a glass of milk **near** the fireplace.

For Rudolph, she left some reindeer treats **near** the window.

She wanted to see Santa arrive so she placed a video camera **near** the Christmas tree.

Tanya fell asleep, but Santa left a great big teddy bear **near** her pillow.

At the Baby Sitter

Skylar stayed with his baby sitter after school. He **never** played with the blocks.

Skylar **never** played in the sandbox.

You would **never** see Skylar on the swings.

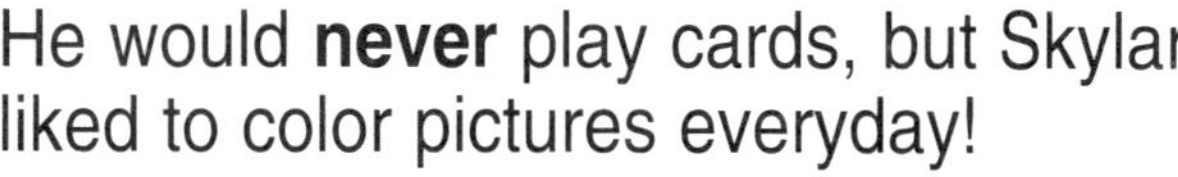

He would **never** play cards, but Skylar liked to color pictures everyday!

Cut on dotted line

Heidi

Heidi **never** got upset. She was always cheerful.

She **never** forgot to raise her hand when she had something to say in class.

She **never** tried to break into the front of the lunch line.

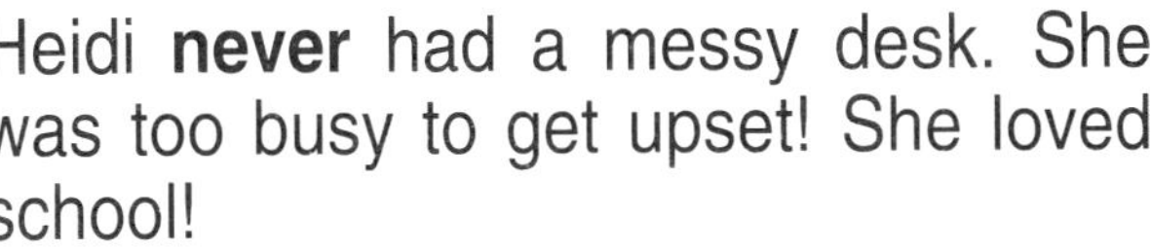

Heidi **never** had a messy desk. She was too busy to get upset! She loved school!

Cut on dotted line

A Mother's Day Gift

Bobby wanted to give his Mom a picture of himself for Mother's Day. First, he stood **next to** a tree.

Then he stood **next to** a cowboy statue.

Bobby had a great idea! He would have a picture of himself taken **next to** his Mom.

Bobby's Mom hung the picture **next to** the fireplace.

Cut on dotted line

Cut on dotted line

Buster Gets Loose

Buster Bunny got out of his cage. He first hopped **next to** a bicycle.

Then he jumped **next to** a flower bed.

He hopped a bit further and relaxed **next to** a bush.

When Buster was **next to** the picnic table, his owner Suzie saw him. Buster's big adventure was over.

All Alone

Miranda the Mouse was all alone. **None** of her Mouse family or friends were at home.

Miranda was hungry for something to eat. She looked for cookies, but **none** were in the jar.

She checked for cheese, but **none** was in the refrigerator.

She wanted crackers, but **none** were in the pantry. Fortunately, her parents came home soon with some snacks.

1 2 3 4

Cut on dotted line

Craig Needs a Pencil

Craig needed a pencil for his homework. He looked in his pencil pouch, but there were **none**.

He checked his backpack but there were **none** there either.

When Craig looked in his desk, he saw he had **none**.

Craig's Mom looked in her purse and found **none**. But, Craig's Dad found a pencil in his briefcase.

Cut on dotted line

Frisky Loves to Jump

Frisky the Dog loved to jump **off** furniture. Every morning, Frisky would jump **off** the bed.

After his nap, he would jump **off** the couch.

Frisky even jumped **off** the big chair.

At the end of the day, Frisky's owner, Travis, took **off** Frisky's collar and gave him a big hug!

Cut on dotted line

Cut on dotted line

Home From School

Kaylin took her backpack **off** as she walked into her house.

She took **off** her coat and gloves too.

She opened the refrigerator and grabbed a soda. She took **off** the bottle cap and poured the soda into a glass.

Kaylin headed for the couch and kicked **off** her shoes. She was glad to be home from school!

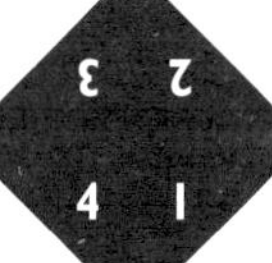

Cut on dotted line

Going Out to Eat

Kyle went into his favorite restaurant. He took **off** his raincoat and cap before he sat down.

He ordered a hamburger, fries, and a milkshake. Kyle took the lid **off** his milk shake and put in a straw.

Kyle took the lid **off** the mustard bottle and poured it on his hamburger.

When Kyle was finished, the waitress cleared **off** the table. Going out to eat was a treat!

www.superduperinc.com • 1-800-277-8737

Cut on dotted line

Mr. Taylor Relaxes

Mr. Taylor took **off** his hat and tie as he walked into the house.

He then slipped **off** his jacket and hung it in the closet.

He grabbed the mail **off** the counter and went to sit down on the couch.

It was nice to relax at the end of the day! Mr. Taylor took the phone **off** the hook!

Going to Camp

Even though it was early, Kellie had to **open** her eyes and jump out of bed.

She walked to her dresser and began to **open** the drawers. She picked out some clothes to pack.

She had to **open** her suitcase and carefully put her clothes inside.

Then she went to **open** her backpack in order to fill it with yummy treats. She was ready for camp!

2 3
1 4

Cut on dotted line

Rusty Wants Breakfast

Every morning, Rusty would **open** his bedroom door and head to the kitchen.

He would **open** the refrigerator and find something to eat for breakfast.

He saw a leftover pizza box and started to **open** it. Pizza for breakfast sounded great to him!

Rusty's Mom walked in. Oops! She made Rusty **open** a new box of cereal for breakfast.

2 3 1 4

Cut on dotted line

School Begins!

It was the first day of school for Tabitha. She slowly began to **open** the door to her classroom.

When the top of her desk was **open**, she found lots of new books and pencils.

In her **open** lunchbox, she saw her favorite sandwich and a special treat.

Her Mom picked her up at the end of the day. Tabitha needed help to **open** the car door.

1 2 3 4

The Missing Necklace

Irene looked for her lucky necklace everywhere. She had to **open** her jewelry box but couldn't find it!

She looked in her Mom's **open** purse, but she didn't see the necklace there either.

Irene's Dad helped to **open** the garage door, but there was no sign of her necklace.

Irene found her necklace on her closet floor. "It must have fallen out of my **open** coat pocket," she said.

Cut on dotted line

Johnny Gets Glasses

Johnny and his mother rode **on** the bus to the eye doctor's.

At the office, they sat **on** chairs and waited for the doctor.

The doctor said Johnny needed glasses. He put some glasses **on** the counter for Johnny to try **on**.

The doctor patted Johnny **on** the head when he found the perfect pair!

Cut on dotted line

Cut on dotted line

Sammy's Top Hat

Sammy the Snake loved to wear a top hat **on** his head.

When Sammy went out to eat, he wore a tie **on** his tail.

During dinner, he put his top hat **on** the table.

After dinner, Sammy put a tip **on** the table and put the hat back **on** his head.

1 2 3 4

The Mice Make Dinner

Millie and Marty Mouse sat **on** chairs near the kitchen table. "Let's have pizza for dinner," they said.

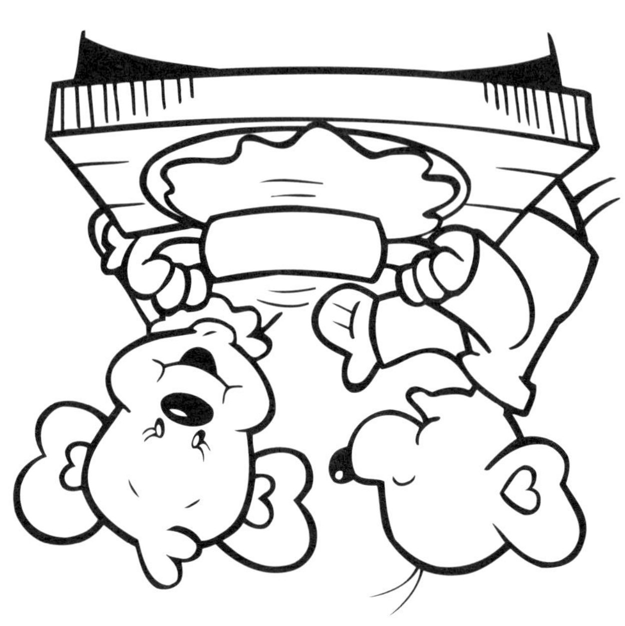

They put a pan **on** the table. Then, they carefully rolled the dough **on** the pan.

Next, they put sauce **on** the dough.

Millie and Marty put shredded cheese **on** the sauce. They couldn't wait for it to cook!

3 2
4 1

Cut on dotted line

Cut on dotted line

Peter skated **on** the ice until his mother called him for dinner.

He put **on** ice skates and carefully stood up.

Peter Ice Skates

Peter took off his skates and put **on** his boots. He carried his skates home **on** his shoulder. What fun!

Peter the Penguin sat **on** the ice.

Perry's Two Friends

Perry the Puppy had two friends. One wore a collar and the **other** wore a coat.

One loved to chase cats while the **other** liked to sleep.

One puppy lived in a doghouse while the **other** lived in the house.

One of the puppies liked canned dog food and the **other** liked dry food. Perry enjoyed both of his friends!

Cut on dotted line

Cut on dotted line

One was holding a ball and the **other** was holding a box.

One had big, black eyes and the **other** had smaller, brown eyes.

2 3
1 4

Patricia's New Teddy

Patricia saw two teddy bears on the toy shelf. One was sitting while the **other** was laying down.

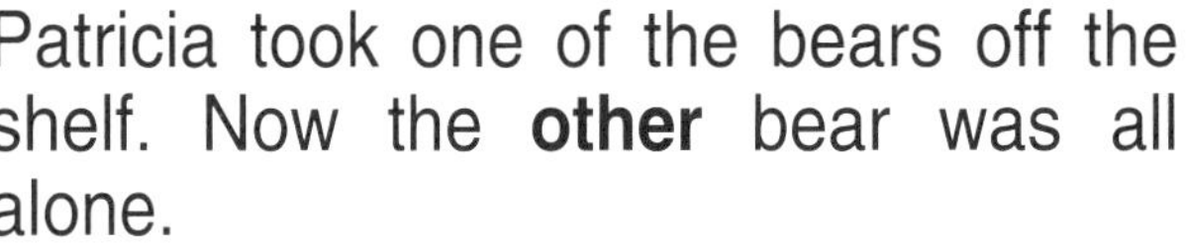

Patricia took one of the bears off the shelf. Now the **other** bear was all alone.

Marvin the Magician

Marvin the Magician jumped **out** of a box to surprise Holly for her birthday.

He began his show by pulling a quarter **out** from behind her ear.

Then he pulled a flower **out** of his pocket and gave it to her.

For his last trick, he pulled a baby bunny **out** of his hat. It was the best birthday Holly ever had!

Cut on dotted line

Cut on dotted line

Police Officer Mike

Police Officer Mike drove up to the school in his squad car. He got **out** of the car.

He walked on stage and spoke to all the boys and girls. He pulled his badge **out** of his wallet.

OfficerMikepulled**out**hisnightstickfrom his belt and showed the students.

Finally, he took **out** a pair of handcuffs from his pocket. What neat stuff!

1 2 3 4

The Family Picnic

Benita and her family were going on a picnic. She took the picnic basket **out** of the cupboard.

Benita then pulled a blanket **out** of the closet.

Her Mom asked her to take the sandwiches **out** of the refrigerator.

Benita's brother grabbed the ice cream **out** of the freezer. The family was ready to go!

Cut on dotted line

Surf's Up!

Kennedy drove his jeep to the beach. He pulled his surf board and beach bag **out** of the jeep.

He took his towel **out** of his beach bag and spread it on the sand.

He took his keys **out** of his pocket and put them in the bag.

Kennedy rode the waves until it was dark. He was sad to get **out** of the water!

Cut on dotted line

1 2 3 4

Going to the Zoo

It was time to go to the zoo. Solomon opened the door and went **outside** of his house.

On his way to the zoo, he dropped two letters in the mailbox **outside** the post office.

When he arrived at the zoo, he stood **outside** the gate until the zoo opened.

As he walked around the zoo, Solomon stood **outside** the cages and looked at the animals.

Fourth of July

It was the Fourth of July and Jeff's family placed a flag **outside** their house.

Jeff decorated the **outside** windows with pictures and streamers.

Before all the fireworks started, Jeff put a row of chairs **outside** on the lawn.

The neighborhood children played **outside** while they waited for the fireworks to begin.

Cut on dotted line

Cut on dotted line

Jumping Jimmy

Jimmy the Cricket loved to jump **over** things.

On sunny days, he jumped **over** tall blades of grass.

When it rained, he jumped **over** mud puddles.

At night, he jumped into bed and his Mom pulled the covers **over** his body up to his neck.

2 3
1 4

Mindy Takes a Swim

Mindy the Monkey loved to swing **over** the river.

One day, she fell in the river and saw some fish swimming **over** her head.

Mindy swam **over** some rocks to get to the other side of the river.

Mindy's Mom picked her out of the river and carried her **over** her shoulder all the way home.

Harvey's Fun Day

Harvey the Horse jumped **over** the fence.

He leaped **over** a row of bushes.

Harvey stopped to eat some apples that hung **over** his head.

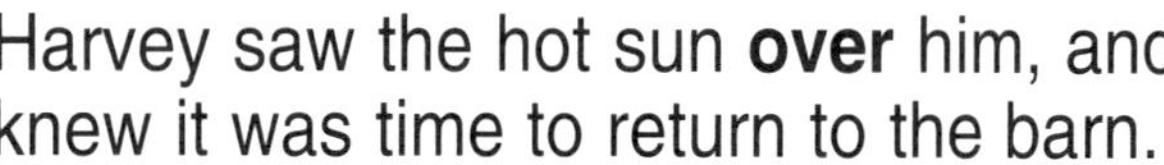
Harvey saw the hot sun **over** him, and knew it was time to return to the barn.

Cut on dotted line

Cut on dotted line

Greg Races Go-carts

Greg loved to race go-carts! He wore a helmet and special goggles **over** his eyes. Vroom!

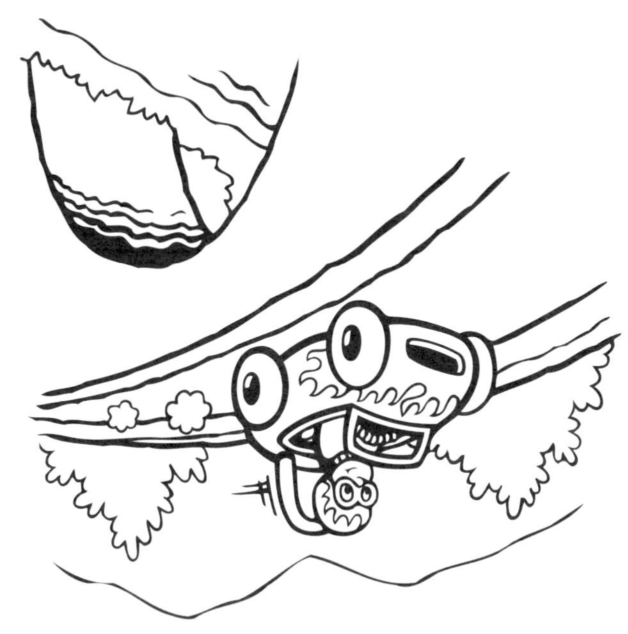

Greg raced **over** a bridge!

He drove **over** the finish line in record time!

A blimp flying **over** Greg took video pictures of the race for television. What a finish!

When she arrived at school, she noticed her best friend Sally was wearing a new **pair** of funny earrings.

She then wore a **pair** of shoes on the wrong feet.

April Fool's Day

It was April Fool's Day. Gloria wanted to do something silly. She giggled as she put her **pair** of socks on inside-out.

"Great!" she said. "Today we can be a **pair** of silly girls."

Cut on dotted line

Getting Ready to Ski

Tanisha went to the ski shop. She bought a new **pair** of skis.

To keep warm, she bought a **pair** of fuzzy mittens.

She found a **pair** of boots with butterfly designs all over them. Tanisha bought those as well.

Tanisha also picked out a **pair** of poles. She was ready to hit the slopes!

A Good Day for Trisha

Trisha had a good day. She knitted a **part** of her new sweater.

She ate **part** of her pizza and shared the rest with her brother.

She colored **part** of her picture, and left the rest of it for tomorrow.

At night before bed, she read a **part** of her book before going to sleep.

Cut on dotted line

Joseph Eats Lunch

Joseph was hungry for lunch. He put **part** of a sandwich and **part** of a pickle on a plate.

He was still hungry so he sliced an apple into four pieces and ate **part** of it.

Joseph wanted something sweet for dessert. He ate a small **part** of a chocolate pie.

After lunch, Joseph ran to the basement and built **part** of his model airplane.

Cut on dotted line

Pirate's Costume

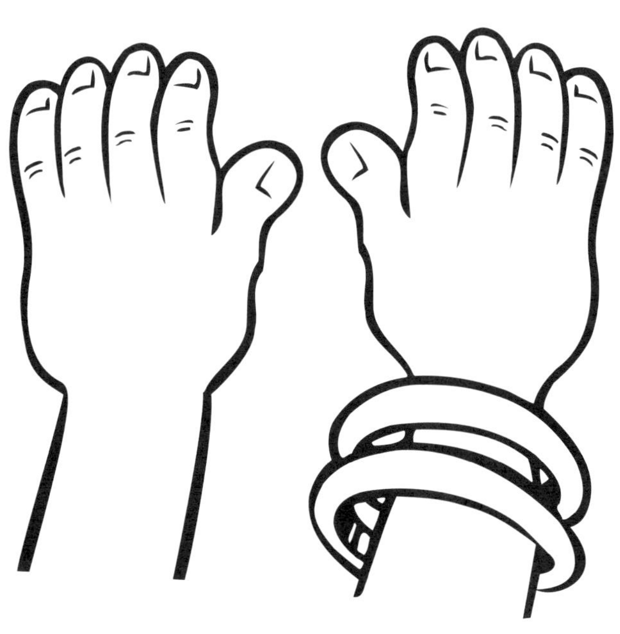

Shalisa dressed up as a pirate for a costume party. She put two bracelets on her **right** arm.

Then she placed a hoop earring on her **right** ear.

She tilted her pirate's hat to the **right**. Shalisa needed something else.

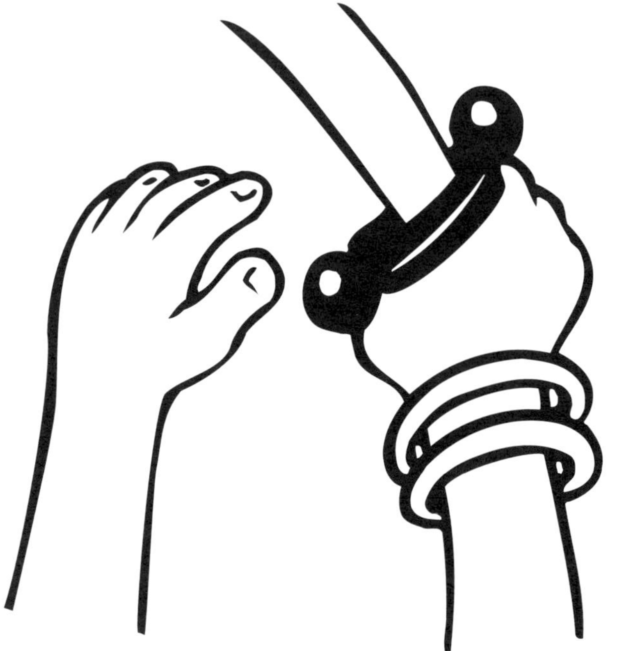

She went to her brother's room and found a plastic sword she could carry in her **right** hand.

Where Is It?

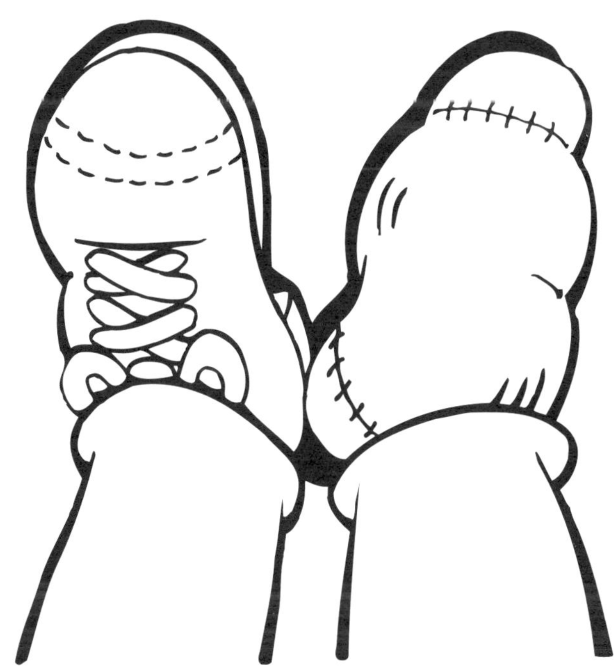

Rocky lost his **right** shoe. He couldn't find it anywhere!

He looked under his bed and found his **right** glove, but no **right** shoe.

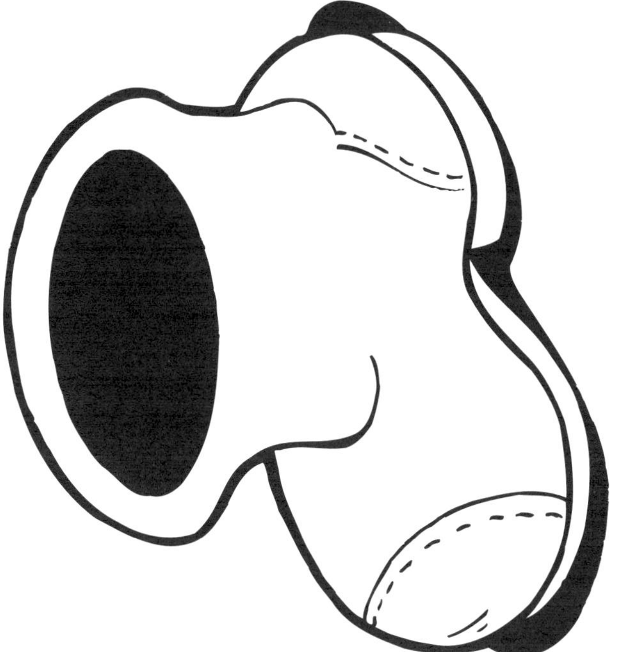

He looked in the closet and found his **right** boot, but still no **right** shoe.

Then, Rocky's little brother ran by wearing the shoe on his **right** foot. Pretty silly!

Cut on dotted line

Willy and Billy

Willy and Billy liked the **same** things. Every Monday, they wore the **same** shirts to school.

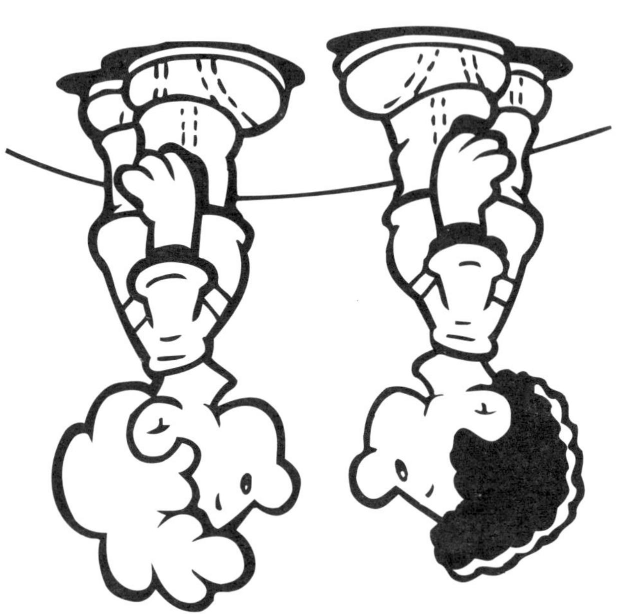

They wore the **same** pants and the **same** hiking boots, too.

At lunch, they always ate the **same** kind of sandwich, peanut butter with grape jelly.

When their teacher asked a question in class, both boys even raised their hands at the **same** time.

Cut on dotted line

1 2 3 4

Cut on dotted line

Terri's Birthday Party

At Terri's birthday party, everyone wore the **same** type of party hat.

They each were given the **same** type of party whistle to blow.

Every child played the **same** game, Pin the Tail on the Donkey.

At the end, everyone received a goodie bag with the **same** type of candy and toys. Great party!

Sharing the Same Things

Sabra had much in common with her classmates. She and her best friend, Donna, had the **same** backpacks.

Sabra and Joey had the **same** type of lunch boxes.

When Sabra rode to school in the morning, she noticed Darla had the **same** style of bike as hers.

Even Toni had the **same** type of raincoat as Sabra!

1 2 3 4

✂ Cut on dotted line

#BK-278 Fold & Say® Basic Concept Stories ©1999 Super Duper® Publications
www.superduperinc.com • 1-800-277-8737

Cut on dotted line

Shopping

Christopher and Trevor went shopping. The two boys bought the **same** type of swimsuits.

In the toy store, they both purchased the **same** style of beachballs.

Christopher and Trevor found the **same** style of beach towels at the department store.

The two boys wanted the **same** goggles and flippers, too. They were ready for the beach!

The New Movie

A new dinosaur movie came to town. Davy was **second** in line to buy a ticket.

He sat in the **second** row so he could see the screen easily.

Davy ordered popcorn before the movie started. He bought a **second** bag of popcorn for his best friend.

After the movie, Davy found his Mom parked in the **second** row of the parking lot.

Second Grade

Breanna was in **second** grade. She sat in the **second** desk from the teacher.

Breanna loved to run races around the track. She stood in the **second** lane ready to run.

The teacher blew her whistle. Breanna ran as hard as she could and came in **second** place.

Breanna was so hungry from all the running that she asked for a **second** hot dog at lunch. Whew!

Cut on dotted line

Jesse Separates Toys

Jesse had a job in a toy store. He had to **separate** the puzzles from the games.

When the dolls and robots were put in a pile, it was his job to **separate** them.

One day a box of action figures, jump ropes, and yo-yo's came in. Jesse worked hard to **separate** the toys.

When the bikes and scooters got mixed up, he had to **separate** them. He liked everything organized.

Cut on dotted line

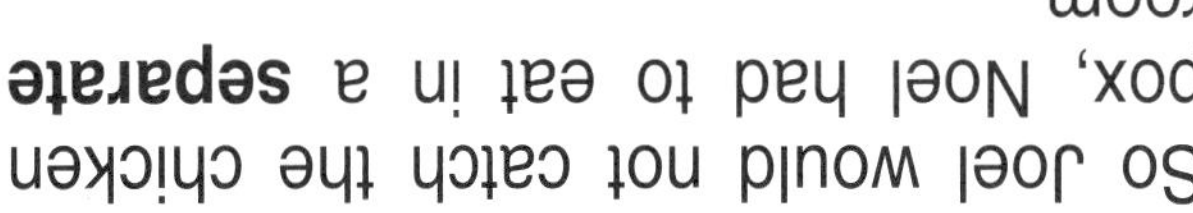

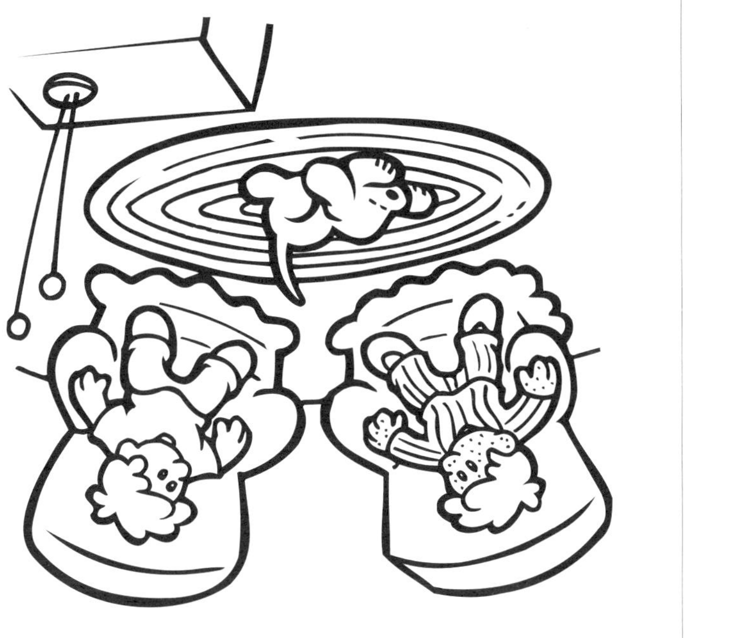

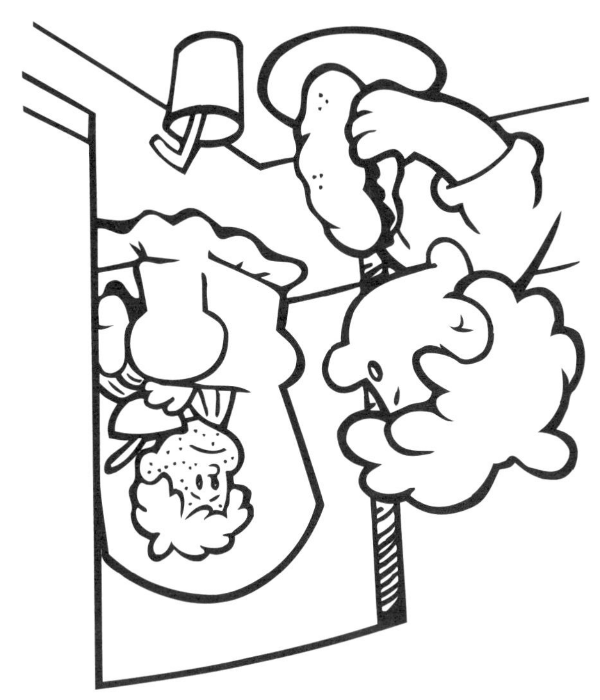

2 3
1 4

Noel and Joel

Their Mom tried to keep the boys **separate** from each other, but Joel still caught the chicken pox!

Noel and Joel shared everything. One day, Noel came down with chicken pox, and had to sleep in a **separate** bed.

Morgan's Recital

It was the morning of Morgan's dance recital. First, she put on a **short** slip.

Then, Morgan put on a **short** dress.

Later, Morgan stopped at the hair salon and decided to have her hair cut **short** too.

Before she went on stage, Morgan put on some **short** earrings. She was ready to dance!

Cut on dotted line

Building a Nest

Roxanne Robin found a **short** branch on the tree to build her nest.

Roxanne needed materials to build her nest and spotted a pile of twigs. She put together some **short** twigs.

Roxanne needed more materials and found **short** bits of string on the sidewalk.

Once she was finished, Roxanne put a **short** feather in her nest for luck. What a cool nest!

Cut on dotted line

Short Can Be Great!

Carmen liked her nickname "**Short** Stuff." Compared to a rocking chair, Carmen was **short**.

When standing at her backyard gate, Carmen looks **short**.

Standing next to the kitchen table, everyone could see Carmen was **short**.

Carmen loved being the **short** one in her family because she could always hide in the smallest places.

Cut on dotted line

Cut on dotted line

Chuck the Chipmunk

In the rain forest, Chuck the Chipmunk was considered a **short** animal.

His friend Ricky Raccoon stood beside him and said, "You are **short**."

Ollie Owl flew over Chuck and hooted, "You are **short**."

Scottie Skunk put his arm around Chuck. He said, "You are **short** and I'm glad you are my friend."

Steve the Bus is Slow

Steve the Bus was **slow**. Cars went past him quickly.

He tried to go faster, but he was still **slow**. Trucks zoomed by him.

Even motorcycles passed by Steve. "Why am I so **slow**?" asked Steve.

"So you can ride with us," said the bicycle riders. "We are **slow** too!"

1 2 3 4

Cut on dotted line

Cut on dotted line

Sylvia is a Slowpoke

Sylvia the centipede was a **slow** centipede.

She was **slow** to put on her shoes.

She was **slow** when she ate leaves.

Her favorite time of the day was when she took a **slow** bath. How refreshing!

Taylor Turtle

Taylor the Turtle was very **slow**.

He walked a **slow** walk while the other animals ran.

He was **slow** when he drew pictures, but his drawings were always the best!

"I may be **slow**," said Taylor, "but, I always finish what I start."

Cut on dotted line

Cut on dotted line

Colton Takes a Trip

Colton rode to his Uncle's house on a **slow** train.

The train had to **slow** down even more when it came to a railroad crossing.

While the train was stopped, Colton looked out the window and saw some **slow** birds flying by.

"When we go on a **slow** trip," the birds said, "we get to enjoy the scenery."

Cut on dotted line

A Very Tall Giant

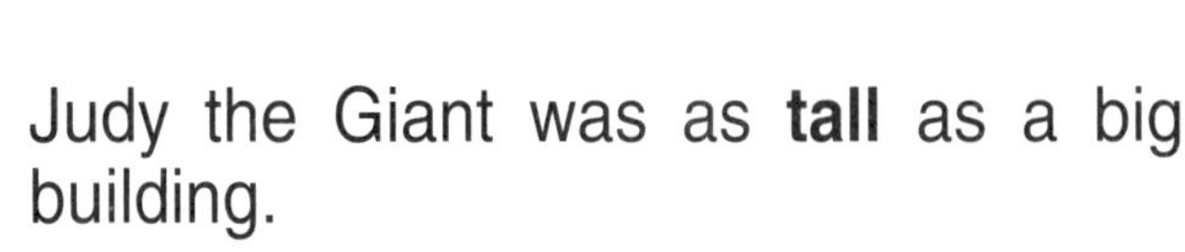

Judy the Giant was as **tall** as a big building.

She was as **tall** as a big hill.

She was even as **tall** as the trees in the forest!

One day Judy met Jerry the Giant. He was as **tall** as Judy, and they became good friends!

Cut on dotted line

Gigi the Giraffe

Gigi the Giraffe was a **tall** giraffe.

At lunch, she would eat leaves from a **tall** tree without having to stretch her neck.

At recess, Gigi always played basketball because she was as **tall** as the basketball hoop.

At night, Gigi even dreamed about **tall** things, like telephone poles and silos on a farm!

1 2 3 4

Harvey the Hippo

Harvey the Hippo went to his favorite restaurant for lunch. He ordered a **thick**, juicy, veggie burger.

Harvey was still hungry, so he ordered a big, **thick**, club sandwich.

Suddenly, he felt a bit thirsty and ordered a **thick** milkshake.

Before leaving the restaurant, Harvey couldn't resist ordering a **thick** slice of chocolate cake.

Cut on dotted line

Barry's New Friend

Barry the Bear had very **thick** fur to keep him warm in the winter.

One day, Barry took a walk through the **thick** forest.

He came upon a lion with a **thick** mane. Barry introduced himself and invited the lion back to his cave.

In the cave they drew pictures with **thick** crayons and snacked on a **thick** stack of pancakes!

Kendra's Bike Ride

Kendra rode on a bike with **thin** tires.

On her way, she chewed on a **thin** piece of gum.

On her head, she wore a hat with a **thin** brim.

She stopped to rest under a leafy tree, and watched the tall, **thin** grass sway by the lake.

Cut on dotted line

A Martian at the Deli

Mark the Martian went to the deli for his favorite sandwich. First he chose two **thin** slices of bread.

Mark then asked for three pieces of roast beef sliced very **thin**.

On top of the roast beef he wanted a very **thin** slice of cheese.

Mark asked for a **thin** slice of tomato, too! He took his sandwich back to his spaceship and flew off.

Cut on dotted line

Carla's Treat

Carla walked home from her friend's house. Her house was the **third** house on the street.

Carla pulled a key chain out of her pocket. Her house key was the **third** key on the chain.

Carla walked in the house and placed her backpack on the **third** shelf of the bookcase.

Carla's Mom had a double scoop ice cream cone waiting for her. Carla was so hungry she added a **third** scoop!

Cut on dotted line

Bobby Blue Jay

Bobby Blue Jay went to flying school. He raced the other blue jays in his class and came in **third** place.

Bobby was excited and he quickly flew home to tell his parents. He lived in the **third** birdhouse from the school.

Bobby's parents were so proud that they served him a **third** worm for dinner.

Bobby even had a **third** slice of insect pie for dessert. Bobby Blue Jay was one happy bird!

Going to the Circus

John and his family went to the circus. Wow! He saw the tiger jump **through** a hoop.

John covered his eyes when the acrobats arrived. He peeked **through** his fingers to watch the acrobats fly.

Later, a trained poodle in a ballerina outfit jumped **through** two hula hoops.

John laughed at the clowns crawling **through** the barrels. John loved the circus!

Cut on dotted line

Cut on dotted line

Booboo the Ghost

Booboo was a friendly ghost who loved to go **through** things. He would fly **through** walls.

He would run **through** the doors.

Booboo would skip **through** closets.

Booboo's favorite thing to walk **through** was his refrigerator. He loved how cool it felt!

Two Walking Buddies

Kathy and Ann loved to walk. The two friends would begin by walking **through** their doorway.

They walked **through** beautiful parks.

They walked **through** grassy fields.

On rainy days, the two would walk **through** the huge mall and window shop. They loved walking.

1 2 3 4

Cut on dotted line

Cut on dotted line

Sparky's Playground

Sparky the Dog wanted to go to the playground. On the way, he jumped **through** a tire hanging from a tree.

Sparky then ran **through** a neighbor's vegetable garden.

Later, he walked **through** lawn sprinklers to cool off.

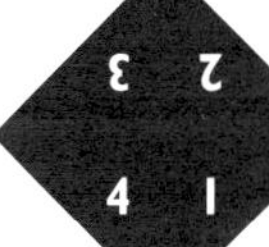

Sparky finally arrived at the playground in time to go **through** the tunnel slides with his dog buddies.

Camping Together

The Biddle family rode **together** in their van to go camping.

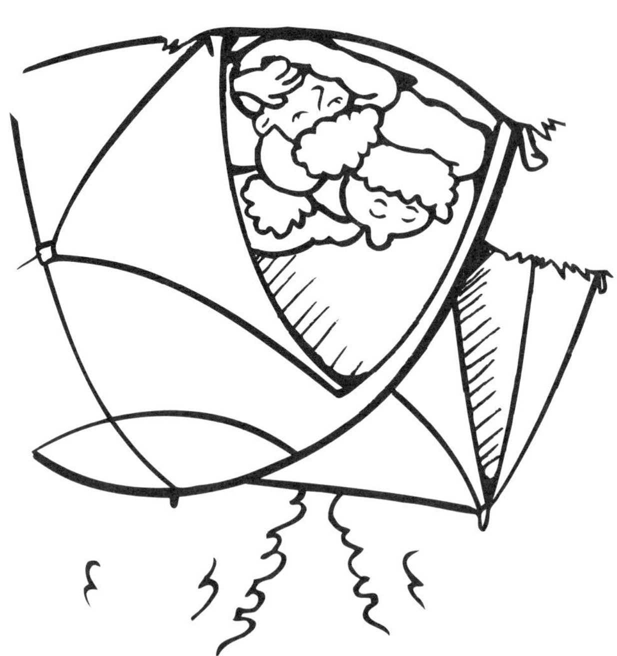

When they arrived, they put up two tents. The kids slept **together** in the round tent.

Mom and Dad Biddle slept **together** in the other tent.

Every night they built a fire and roasted hot dogs and marshmallows **together**.

Cut on dotted line

Thanksgiving

Nancy invited her family over for Thanksgiving. She put their coats **together** in the closet.

She placed the purses and hats **together** on her bed.

All the children put puzzles **together** in the basement.

Nancy rang a small bell and everyone sat **together** at the table ready to eat a delicious dinner.

Luis went into the bathroom and took the **top** off the toothpaste. He brushed his teeth and washed his face too.

Luis climbed to the **top** bunk and crawled under his sheets.

2 3
1 4

Bedtime

Luis was getting ready for bed. He pulled his pajamas out of the **top** drawer of his dresser.

His Mom came in and kissed him on the **top** of his head. "Sweet dreams!" his Mom said.

Cut on dotted line

Cut on dotted line

Slim the Snake

Slim the Snake put a hat on **top** of his head and went out the door.

Slim slowly slithered to the post office. He crawled up to the **top** of the flagpole.

He then jumped on **top** of a friendly postal worker's sack. The two of them left to deliver the mail.

On the way, Slim sat on **top** of some magazines in his seat so he could see out the window.

Timmy Loses a Tooth

Timmy the Monkey lost his first tooth while munching on a banana. At first, he put the tooth **under** his hat.

At lunch, he carefully put his tooth **under** his napkin.

When he went to class, Timmy placed his tooth **under** some papers in his desk.

That night, Timmy slid his tooth **under** his pillow. The next morning, he found two ripe bananas from the tooth fairy!

2 3
1 4

Cut on dotted line

Cut on dotted line

Sarah Hides For Fun!

Sarah the Shy Snake loved to hide **under** things. She often hid **under** branches and twigs.

Sometimes she hid **under** big bushes.

Sarah loved the fall because she could hide **under** the piles of pretty leaves.

Sarah's Mom called, "Sarah, time to come home! You can hide **under** more things tomorrow!"

Under the Umbrella

It was a rainy day and Abigail stood outside **under** her umbrella.

Her best friend Samantha was standing **under** a newspaper. "Come join me," invited Abigail.

Later, the girls saw Gabriel standing **under** the bridge. "Is there room for me **under** the umbrella?" he asked.

"Sure!" answered Abigail. The three friends walked to Abigail's house **under** the big umbrella and kept dry.

Cut on dotted line

Cut on dotted line

Dede Loves to Dig

Dede the Gopher liked to dig holes all over town. She dug holes **under** houses.

Dede dug holes **under** schools.

She even dug holes **under** park slides.

One day while digging **under** a tree, Dede met Al the Gopher. The two friends now dig their holes together!

Balloon Ride

David zipped **up** his jacket before going on his first hot air ballon ride.

He climbed **up** the ladder and jumped inside the basket.

Up, **up**, **up** into the sky the hot air balloon flew.

David flew **up** and over the trees, birds, and even clouds! He took lots of pictures to show his family.

Cut on dotted line

Celeste's Kite

It was a windy day and Celeste ran **up** the stairs to get her kite.

Her kite was **up** on the top shelf, so she needed to get a ladder.

Celeste climbed **up** the ladder and pulled down her beautiful butterfly kite.

She ran outside and had the kite **up** in the air in no time! Celeste loved windy days!

Climbing a Mountain

Beau got **up** from the bed and couldn't wait to go climbing.

He found his climbing gear **up** in the attic.

Beau saw his hiking boots high **up** in a box in the garage.

He was all set! He drove to the mountains, and climbed **up** to the very top!

Cut on dotted line

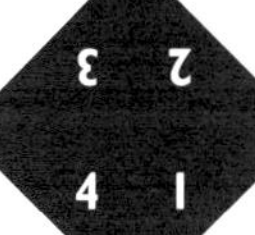

Abdul's Birthday

Abdul jumped **up** from his chair. Today he was having his birthday party!

Abdul put away all the toys in his bedroom and placed them **up** on the shelves.

Abdul helped his Mom with the party balloons. They floated **up** high near the ceiling.

Abdul's Mom hung **up** streamers around the windows and doors. Abdul was ready for the party!

Cut on dotted line

A Day With Dad

Donna's Dad spent the **whole** day with her today. They began by riding bikes around the **whole** lake.

Donna was thirsty after the ride and drank a **whole** bottle of water.

Donna and her Dad then rode to the ice cream shop. They each ate a **whole** banana split!

When they got home, Donna's Dad read her a **whole** comic book. The day with Dad was wonderful!

Cut on dotted line

A Very Hungry Mouse

Morris the Mouse was just beginning to eat a **whole** cheesecake. He loved cheesecake!

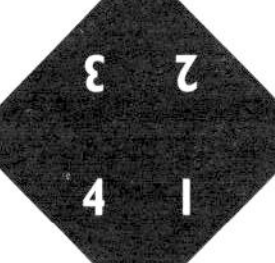

Morris was a growing mouse, so he also ate a **whole** box of cheese and crackers!

Then, Morris began to drink a **whole** bottle of root beer. It was very fizzy.

Morris was still hungry, so his mother gave him a **whole** pickle and a **whole** watermelon. Yummy!

My Fold and Say Book

by:________________________________

(name)

My Fold and Say Book

by:________________________________

(name)